A

SOUTHERN FAMILY

IN WHITE AND BLACK

NUMBER THIRTEEN
Texas A&M Southwestern Studies

A Southern

Family

in

White & Black

THE CUNEYS OF TEXAS

Douglas Hales

Texas A&M University Press • College Station

Library of Congress Cataloging-in-Publication Data

Hales, Douglas, 1951–
    A southern family in white and black : the Cuneys of Texas /
Douglas Hales.—1st ed.
        p. cm.—(Texas A & M southwestern studies ; no. 13)
    Includes bibliographical references and index.
    ISBN 1-58544-200-3 (alk. paper)
    1. Cuney family.   2. Cuney, Norris Wright, 1846–
1898.   3. African Americans—Biography.   4. Racially mixed
people—United States—Biography.   5. African American
politicians—Texas—Biography.   6. Texas—Politics and government—1865–1950.   7. Texas—Race relations.   8. Cuney,
Philip Minor, b. 1807.   9. Cuney-Hare, Maud, 1874–1936.
10. Texas—Biography.   11. Austin County (Tex.)—
Biography.   1. Title.   11. Series.
E185.96 .H185   2003
976.4004'96073'00922—dc21   2002007553

CONTENTS

ILLUSTRATIONS

PREFACE

In 1964 Ralph Ellison criticized what he saw as scholarly misperceptions of African American history and culture: "Prefabricated Negroes are sketched on sheets of paper and superimposed upon the Negro community; then when someone thrusts his head through the pages and yells, 'Watch out there, Jack, there's people living under here,' they are all shocked and indignant." Ellison's remarks reflected the state of black history and the demands of many involved in the civil rights movement of the 1960s. African Americans no longer accepted second-class citizenship, racial stereotypes, or their exclusion from American history books. By the late 1960s and early 1970s, colleges and universities finally heeded the demands of black activists and began developing courses on African American history and black studies programs. Since then, perceptions of African Americans and their history have radically changed and have had a significant effect on the scholarly understanding of American history.

One aspect of the black experience that historians have only recently begun to explore is the African American elite of the late nineteenth and early twentieth centuries. The majority of these people were the mulatto descendants of white antebellum planters or northern free blacks. This book explores the lives of Philip Minor Cuney, a white planter and Texas politician; Norris Wright Cuney, his mulatto son and successful leader of the Republican party in Texas; and Maud Cuney-Hare, the daughter of Wright Cuney and a noted concert pianist, musicologist, and author.

Wright Cuney and his daughter represent two types of African American elites. Coming out of slavery as an educated mulatto, Wright Cuney clearly had advantages over other black freedmen. His light complexion, education, and background allowed Cuney to become a member of a small black political leadership during Reconstruction. Afterward, Cuney continued in this role but also became part of a growing black middle-class. Like many other middle-class African Americans, he assumed a larger role within the black community by pursuing the social betterment of his race. Maud Cuney-Hare represents the second generation of African American elites following slavery. Facing disfranchisement and segregation in the South, Cuney-Hare like others moved to the North. Excluded from the political process, she and others sought the betterment of their race through education and the arts. In many respects Cuney-Hare epitomizes W. E. B. Du Bois's idea of the "talented tenth."

This study begins with Philip Cuney. He had much in common with other paternalistic slaveholders of the South. He believed in the institution of slavery and had grown accustomed to the lifestyle that the peculiar institution afforded him. By Texas standards, his expansive tracts of land and large number of slaves made him a wealthy man. He became a respected and prominent leader in Austin County and also went into Texas politics, enjoying some success both before and after Texas became a state. Cuney, like many southern planters, used his powerful position as a slaveholder to begin a sexual relationship with one of his female slaves, Adeline Stuart, which produced eight mulatto children. Along with his white wife and children, Cuney in effect had two families, one white and one black.

During his lifetime, Philip Cuney witnessed great changes for his society. He participated in the annexation of Texas to the United States and saw both slavery and cotton become dominant factors in both the antebellum economy and southern life. He watched the United States divide between North and South and devolve into Civil War. Before his death in 1866, he endured the destruction of his way of life and his slaves' emancipation. In an ironic twist of history, Philip Cuney would be less remembered for his political career or for his success as a planter than as a white father who chose to free his slave children, including Norris Wright Cuney. Clearly, Philip Cuney differed from the majority of other planters. This study will attempt to explain the differences, including the extent of the relationship between Philip and Adeline and why he manumitted and then educated his mulatto children.

Wright Cuney, Philip's fourth child, who was a bright and physically attractive man of olive complexion, returned to Texas following the Civil War, determined to make the most of his new status as a free man. He dedicated his life to his family, his city, to Republican politics, and to his people. During his lifetime, he also saw enormous changes take place. Following the Civil War, Congress accorded African Americans their citizenship and civil rights. In the process of reconstruction, blacks began to exercise their rights through the ballot and elective office. They organized their own churches, found lost loved ones sold during slavery, formed families, and created their own communities. After Reconstruction, the federal government abandoned its obligations toward African Americans and left them to face the enmity of southern whites. In the face of white hostility, black southerners saw their civil rights slowly erode as the former Confederate states, through violence and law, disfranchised black voters. Through it all, Wright Cuney rose to positions of economic and political leadership and fought to keep African Americans as participants in society.

Following Reconstruction, Wright Cuney, became leader of the Republican Party in Texas. In 1888 he proved instrumental in obtaining black support for Benjamin Harrison's successful bid for the presidency. Cuney added to his powerful presence in the state when Harrison appointed him to the most sought-after federal position, collector of customs at Galveston. Through this post, Cuney obtained the power to distribute federal patronage to both whites and blacks. As the most powerful African American in Texas, and arguably in the entire South, Wright Cuney became the focal point of white hostility. Besides facing animosity from Democrats, he faced an insurgent "Lily White" movement from within his own party. Because of Cuney's effective leadership, blacks in Texas remained a powerful force within the Republican Party, while in many other southern states the party of Lincoln repudiated African Americans. In Galveston, Cuney won election to the city council and distinguished himself as a civic leader. He became an influential spokesman for African American education. On the Galveston docks, Cuney organized blacks into a labor union and challenged the domination of white workers. The following chapters will explore how he gained political experience and maintained his leadership position, analyzing the reasons for his successes and defeats in labor-business negotiations and in local politics.

Wright Cuney's daughter, Maud, followed a very different course than that of her father, but one no less marked by accomplishment. Compared to most black and many white children of the nineteenth century, she led a privileged life. Maud Cuney lived in a musical household with a father who played the violin and a mother who sang soprano and often performed publicly. Her parents surrounded her and brother Lloyd with fine literature and poetry. Because of Wright Cuney's financial status, she received an elegant education from the New England Conservatory of Music and Harvard's Lowell Institute of Literature. While attending college, she began a close and lifelong friendship with W. E. B. Du Bois, who became a noted black intellectual. After her second marriage, Maud Cuney-Hare moved to Boston permanently and pursued a successful career in the arts. She became a masterful concert pianist, musicologist, and playwright. Cuney-Hare became actively involved in the racial uplift movement of the early twentieth century. The culmination of her career came with the publication of her historical study *Negro Musicians and Their Music.*

In the North, she became part of an African American elite that had a dramatic influence on black history. While blacks languished in almost apartheid conditions in the South, African American education and culture made tremendous advances in northern cities. New organizations like the National Association for the Advancement of Colored People and African American women's clubs formed to combat lynching, disfranchisement, and segregation. Black newspapers exposed white racism and violence. African American intellectuals, writers, artists, and musicians led the cultural and historical awakening of black America that culminated in the Harlem Renaissance of the 1920s. Through her music, writing, and other artistic endeavors, Maud Cuney-Hare made a significant contribution to that awakening. The latter chapters of this work will explore her decision against "passing" as white and her commitment to uplift before discussing whether her cultural contributions remained strictly middle class or went beyond that viewpoint.

This book looks at three generations of the Cuney family through 129 years of American history. Each generation influenced the next. Philip, Wright, and Maud Cuney also encountered influences from other people and from the society in which they lived.

ACKNOWLEDGMENTS

There is a long list of people I am indebted to for their help and assistance in creating this study. First is Alwyn Barr at Texas Tech University, who first suggested the topic and provided expert advice and criticism. This book would not have been possible without his encouragement and guidance. I would also like to thank Paul Carlson of Texas Tech. His encouragement and assistance were invaluable. I will be forever grateful to these two fine scholars and professors.

The research process for this study was long and difficult, taking me to four states and to the District of Columbia. There are many people and libraries to thank for their assistance with this. First on the list is Barbara Lawrence, the city secretary of Galveston, and her two assistants, Terry R. Dennis-Williams and Charmaine Wright. I repeatedly interrupted their busy schedules on my trips to and from the city vault accessing 120-year-old city records. Thanks also go to Wayne T. De Cesar, archivist at the National Archives in Washington, D.C. He led me through several miles of archival manuscripts to find long-forgotten appointment papers from 1888. A special thanks goes to the Woodruff Library Archives, Clark Atlanta University, for access to the manuscript collection of Maud Cuney-Hare. The people at Bennett College at Greenville, North Carolina; Rice University at Houston; the Center for American History at the University of Texas; and the Texas State Library at Austin also provided much appreciated help.

Finally, I owe a special debt of gratitude to my sister, Ginger Bowen. She not only provided financial assistance and encouragement in writing this book but also made it possible for me to leave the private sector and obtain my Ph.D. Thanks also to my brother, David Hales, for additional financial assistance and encouragement and to my friend Mark Damron for his critiques and advice.

A

SOUTHERN FAMILY

IN WHITE AND BLACK

CHAPTER I

Philip Cuney
Politician and Slaveholder

MARY BOYKIN CHESNUT, the wife of a noted Confederate politician, saw firsthand the dark side of slavery and wrote in her diary: "God forgive us, but ours is a monstrous system, a wrong and an iniquity! Like the patriarchs of old, our men live all in one house with their wives and their concubines; and the mulattoes one sees in every family partly resemble the white children." She condemned the practice by some slaveholders of having two families in the antebellum South. Sexual exploitation of female slaves by southern slaveholders represented one of the most heinous aspects of that peculiar institution. The progeny of such affairs presented a special problem for southern society and for the exploitative slaveholder. Whether for reasons of guilt, love, or a combination of the two, slaveholders sometimes freed their illicit offspring. According to Eugene Genovese, "Throughout the history of the slave regime there were planters who openly or surreptitiously accepted responsibility for the paternity of mulattoes, educated them, freed them, and, when manumission became difficult, made special provisions for their care." After a sixteen-year relationship with his female slave Adeline Stuart that resulted in eight children, Philip Minor Cuney of Texas became one of those planters.[1]

Joel Williamson, in his book *New People: Miscegenation and Mulattoes in the United States*, wrote that while miscegenation occurred between all races and classes, the "most dramatic and most significant portion was between upper-class white men of the slaveholding class and mulatto slave women engaged in domestic service." Their relationships defied "the rising inclinations of their society" against such behavior. Williamson identified slaveholders who provided protection and education for their mulatto offspring as "mavericks." Often, maverick slaveholders exhibited a genuine fondness and devotion to their slave families that developed alongside their continued affection for their white family. Usually, the relationship only ended with the death of the slaveholder or slave. Philip Cuney exhibited several characteristics of a slaveholding maverick.[2]

The white Cuney ancestors came to North America from Wales in the late eighteenth century. According to family tradition, Philip's grandmother Louise left England with her young son Richmond Edmund shortly after the imprisonment of her husband for an unknown political offense against the crown. The elder Cuney later died in prison. Louise Cuney first went to French Martinique, where she stayed for a short time, then to New Orleans, arriving sometime before 1780. In Louisiana the widow Cuney married Caesar Archinard, a recent immigrant from Switzerland. Although a foreigner, Archinard received a position as commandant of the Spanish post El Rapido. While there, Archinard received a large land grant from the Spanish government. After the purchase of Louisiana by Pres. Thomas Jefferson, El Rapido became Rapides Parish. The Archinards had one son of their own, John, and prospered in the New World, accumulating much land and many slaves.[3]

Archinard's relationship with Richmond Cuney was a good one; Richmond later named his firstborn son after his stepfather. Archinard also aided the young man with the establishment of his own plantation, which he named "Clio," six miles outside Alexandria, Louisiana. Richmond married Tabitha Wells, the daughter of a prominent and wealthy El Rapido family, in 1794. A close relationship developed between the Wells and Cuney families, both of which became active in Rapides Parish politics. Over the next thirteen years, Tabitha and Richmond had six sons, including Philip, the youngest, who was born on March 15, 1807. All of their children received an education, with two becoming lawyers and one a physician. Following Richmond's death in 1824, Tabitha married Seth Lewis, one of the first judges appointed in Louisiana after it became a territorial possession of the United States.[4]

Like much of the frontier South in the early nineteenth century, the territory of Louisiana outside New Orleans had a tradition of violence and lawlessness. Duels and gunfights became a common occurrence. As new immigrants flooded into the area after the American acquisition, Louisiana became a hotbed of political activity. Older established families like the Cuneys and Wells struggled with newer arrivals for political dominance. Factional politics often became entangled with rapacious land speculation. Speculators often defaulted, leaving local banks holding worthless properties, so that by the 1820s, credit began to tighten up. Bankers often received death threats from disappointed loan applicants and others who lost their properties to foreclosure. In 1824, newer residents supported by banking concerns tried to take over politics in Rapides Parish. In an election replete with charges of fraud on both sides, newcomer Maj. Norris Wright gained election as sheriff. Two years later, the old guard retook the sheriff's office when a Cuney cousin, Samuel Wells, beat Wright.[5]

Elections were hard-fought affairs in this part of Louisiana, and violence often took place during and after campaigns. Any perceived attack on another man's honor frequently led to a duel. One of the most famous involved the Cuney and Wells families, their friend Jim Bowie, and their political adversaries on a Mississippi River sandbar outside Natchez, Mississippi. Fought on September 19, 1827, the duel and its subsequent mayhem resulted in the wounding of two men and the deaths of Philip's brother Samuel Cuney and Norris Wright. Dr. Thomas Maddox, a Norris Wright supporter, had challenged the new sheriff, Samuel Wells, to a duel. What began as a dispute between two political opponents escalated into a bloody affair as nine men, all bitter foes, accompanied the duelists to Natchez. Wells brought along his brother Jefferson, Richard and Gen. Sam Cuney, a man identified as McWhorter, and Jim Bowie. Maddox brought Norris Wright, Gen. A. R. Crain, Alfred and Gary Blanchard, and a surgeon named Dr. Denny. Most of those involved, at one time or another, had disagreements with individuals on the other side. Accounts about this famous confrontation differ, for those involved used the duel as an opportunity to settle old scores. Neither side came out unscathed. The reputations of the Wells and Cuney families and many of the others involved never recovered.[6]

Even though Philip Cuney did not participate, he did have political ambitions of his own. Cuney probably felt he could not realize his ambitions with the duel's legacy and the familial feuds that characterized Rapides Parish and therefore moved to Texas in 1837. Other reasons may have played a role in Philip's relocation. As the youngest of six, he may have felt his opportunities for inheritance limited. His first marriage, in September, 1833, to Carolina Scott, the daughter of a local judge, tragically ended with her sudden death ten months later. Following independence from Mexico, Texas in the late 1830s had become an attractive destination for southern emigration, for the new republic offered cheap and abundant land. These factors probably led Cuney to decide to cross the Sabine River into Texas.

The rolling hills of Austin County, named in honor of Stephen F. Austin and organized in 1837 in southeastern Texas, became Cuney's final destination. He settled ten miles southeast of present-day Hempstead. His plantation consisted of 1,800 acres of prime agricultural land along Iron Creek, a tributary of the Brazos River. Cuney named his plantation "Sunnyside," and through the labor of a large number of slaves, he began to turn the black fertile land into a prosperous farming operation. In 1860 Cuney owned real property valued at $295,000 and personal property of $31,000. No record exists of how or when he began to acquire slaves, but most of them probably came with him to Texas. By 1850, he owned 105 individuals, making him one of the largest slaveholders in the state. His total number of slaves had increased to 115 by 1860.[7]

Like other Texas planters, Cuney grew cotton, but unlike most he also chose to diversify. On his 630 acres of cultivated land, which produced 432 bales of cotton in 1850, Cuney began to grow sweet potatoes and corn. He also began a dairy operation. By 1860, Cuney had 700 head of milk cattle producing five thousand pounds of butter a year. When he married his second wife, Eliza Ware, in 1842, she brought with her an additional 1,200 head of cattle and sixteen work mules that contributed to the profitability of the operation.[8]

Eliza Cuney came from a family of some wealth. Beside the large number of livestock and mules, she brought over $23,000 into the marriage. Cuney used this money and an additional $10,000 he borrowed from William H. Kitchen, a longtime Austin County resident, to speculate in land. By the time of his death in January, 1866, Cuney had acquired an additional 883 acres along the Brazos and one-quarter interest in over 13,000 additional acres, making him one of the largest landowners in the state. But doing this heavily burdened Cuney with debt. As one of the fifty largest slaveowners in Texas, he secured much of his debt with his 105 slaves, a common practice in Texas. Severe labor shortages in the state caused slave values to increase from an average $440 in the 1840s to $765 by 1860. After emancipation and his death in 1866, Cuney left his heirs saddled with over $110,000 in debt. With no slaves and plummeting land prices following the Civil War, his debts exceeded his assets by $90,000.[9]

Until the war and in spite of heavy debt, Cuney prospered. With Eliza he had three children. He built a large "Greek Revival home with large frontal colonnades." By Texas standards, Philip Cuney was a wealthy man. Once financially established, he began to dabble in Texas politics. The Cuney and Wells families in Louisiana supported the Whig Party, and Philip may have sympathized with that persuasion, but following statehood, Cuney joined the Democratic Party. He successfully obtained election to the House of Representatives of the Republic of Texas in 1843. Even though Cuney failed to distinguish himself with any legislative accomplishments in the Texas House, Austin County elected him to the Annexation Convention in 1845.[10]

There Cuney obtained appointment on the Legislative and General Provisions Committees. In creating a new constitution, Cuney's voting pattern reflected a belief in limited government both legislatively and administratively. He voted against giving the governor power over most appointments, including the attorney general, district attorneys, or judges. Cuney wanted limited terms for senators and representatives and voted to limit legislative sessions and to forbid a pay raise for the governor for ten years. In addition, he supported keeping the laws established in the Constitution of 1836 pertaining to slavery. That document had legalized slavery, reversed Mexican laws against slave immigration, and forbidden the state to force slave emancipation. Cuney voted in the majority on an act allowing owners to free their own slaves if the owner so desired. The convention caused some later confusion by not specifically stating whether a freed slave could remain in the state. The Texas Supreme Court eventually ruled in 1854 that "manumission could only occur if the slave was sent outside the state."[11]

Following statehood, Cuney won election to the Texas Senate from Austin and Fort Bend Counties. In 1846 he also won election as brigadier general of the 1st Brigade of the 4th Division of the Texas Militia. If his previous experience had been a political education, then Cuney learned well. He became an active participant in the First and Second Legislatures. He obtained appointment to two standing committees, Military

Affairs and Claims and Accounts, and served as chairman of the latter. Cuney also sat on numerous special committees, including those concerning joint resolutions and legislation. One resolution he introduced began the process of appointing district attorneys for the individual districts of the new state. In the first appointment, Cuney nominated and the Senate approved his friend Hiram G. Waller as district attorney of Austin County. The Waller and Cuney families dominated Austin County politics for most of the nineteenth century. Cuney's son Philip Jr. later married Hiram Waller's daughter and went on to serve several terms in the legislature. Waller became a district judge and, with the younger Cuney, became instrumental in the division of Austin County to create Waller County in 1874.[12]

During the Second Legislature, Cuney continued to be a very active member of the Senate, with appointments to the Public Lands, Education, Internal Improvements, and Contingent Expenses Committees. Cuney, like any good politician, took care of his home district. He introduced and passed a bill for the construction of a turnpike connecting Houston and Austin County. He sponsored legislation authorizing Austin County to take ownership of the property of San Felipe and called for the election of a new county seat. Once the second largest commercial center in Texas, retreating Texas troops had burned San Felipe during the Texas Revolution to keep it out of the hands of the advancing Mexican army. Although incorporated as the county seat of Austin County in 1837, the town never regained its former status. Cuney's bill eventually paved the way for the establishment of a new county seat at Bellville.[13]

Cuney also became involved in controversy. Six days before the legislature was to adjourn, he introduced a resolution calling for the resignation of federal judge John C. Watrous. The controversial jurist had acquired powerful enemies in his adopted state. Born in Connecticut in 1806, Watrous studied law in Tennessee, where he became a friend of James K. Polk. Like Cuney, he moved to Texas in 1837 and became heavily involved in land speculation in Austin County and other areas. He became Texas attorney general in 1838 but resigned in 1840 because of conflicts of interest with speculative concerns he formerly represented. Following annexation, President Polk nominated his old friend to the federal bench, ignoring the wishes of Texas' two U.S. senators, Sam Houston and Thomas J. Rusk; Houston supported A. B. Shelby, a former district judge during the republic era, while Rusk favored former attorney general James Webb.[14]

Cuney was not alone in his opposition to Watrous. Antagonism toward the judge began before his appointment to the federal bench when, as a lawyer, he represented the New York Land Company. The company owned over two million acres in headright certificates that the Texas Supreme Court had declared invalid and fraudulent. On behalf of his client, Watrous filed suit in federal court to try to overturn the Texas court decision but resigned from the case when Polk appointed him to the federal bench. In lieu of legal fees, Watrous received stock in the company. Later he testified in court on behalf of his former client. Though the U.S. Supreme Court upheld the Texas court decision, many believed the actions of Watrous to be improper. In the resolution he introduced, Cuney accused the judge of misusing his judicial influence in an attempt to validate forged land certificates. On the state senate floor, Cuney called Watrous an "alien at heart and enemy to everything Texas, without one feeling in common with the people, whose homes have been established here in days of fearful peril, he has come like a fiend to sit in judgment upon us." Both the Texas Senate and the House of Representatives voted for Watrous's removal. When he refused to resign, the U.S. Congress, at the urging of Sam Houston, began impeachment proceedings. The trial never took place, however, because Congress in 1858 decided to drop the case by a vote of 111 to 97. After Houston left the Senate, Andrew J. Hamilton continued to seek the impeachment of the judge until Congress adjourned in 1861.[15]

Just as he did at the Annexation Convention, Cuney continued to take an active interest in any legislation dealing with slavery. The legislature passed his bill preventing "retailers of spirituous or vinous liquors from providing alcohol to slaves" without written consent of the slaveholder. Another bill that passed the legislature made it "illegal to bring into Texas slaves who had committed high crimes in territories or other states." Cuney sought to protect the investment of slaveholders by sponsoring legislation requiring that at least half of any patrol sent to recapture runaway slaves comprise slaveholders. As a delegate to the 1848 Democratic National Convention, Cuney and the other Texas delegates went committed to support the idea of noninterference in the institution of slavery by other states or by the federal government. While the delegation preferred a southerner to lead the national ticket, the Texans voted for Sen. Lewis Cass of Michigan, who favored such noninterference.[16]

Cuney as a politician and a planter committed his future to the future of slavery. The fact that he used his slaves as collateral for land speculation illustrated an optimistic belief that the peculiar institution would continue to thrive in Texas. He knew his way of life as it then existed could only continue with slave labor. Sunnyside, like most plantations in antebellum Texas, was profitable because of its slaves. According to historian Randolph Campbell, "slavery was the key to an agricultural economy in antebellum Texas that was profitable, self-sufficient in food production, and growing." Fearing that slavery was threatened by the incoming Republican administration of Abraham Lincoln, Cuney, like most Texans in 1861, favored secession from the United States.[17]

The very act of owning another human being for economic gain required the slaveholder to develop an ideology that made slavery acceptable. Philip Cuney left no written record of how he viewed slavery or his role as a slaveowner, but some generalizations are possible from his actions regarding his mulatto offspring. It appears that Cuney, like most slaveholders in the South, considered himself a benevolent master. Paternalism allowed him to rationalize the ownership of slaves as being in the best interest of the slaves. According to historian Herbert G. Gutman, "paternalistic beliefs, which often fostered owner responsibility toward slaves, and racial ideology allowed slaveowners to transfer to themselves the adult capacities revealed to them in day-to-day slave behavior. The belief that the adult slave was either a repressed savage or a manchild legitimized ownership and the exercise of authority as civilizing functions."[18]

Other evidence of Cuney's paternalistic nature may be found in his legislation preventing slaves from getting liquor. Also, a study of his slaveholdings in the Censuses of 1850 and 1860 shows that he kept the same slaves for that ten-year period. The same records show that half of his slave population was over the age of fifty. Such statistics may bear out a genuine attachment to his slave community. While these assumptions may or may not be accurate for his attitudes toward his slaveholdings generally, it does appear to be the case regarding Adeline Stuart, his house servant and the mother of the eight children Cuney fathered.

Adeline Stuart was born in 1818 to Hester Neale Stuart, a slave of Potomac Indian, African American, and Caucasian heritage, who belonged to the Neale family of Alexandria, Virginia. The attractive woman had straight black hair, dark eyes, and a light complexion. When Cuney acquired her is unknown, but their relationship began in 1839, following the death of his first wife and after his move to Texas. Cuney may have followed the practice of many other slaveholders who "purchased comely black women for their concubines." Stuart ran the Cuney household and, with her children, apparently lived within the home. She maintained supervision of her own children, who also worked in the Cuney household. Stuart, according to Maud Cuney-Hare, "was an especially active and industrious little woman who kept everyone about her busy whenever she could find anything for them to do." All of the children resembled their mother in appearance, except her two daughters who favored their father with blue eyes and blond hair. Her second son, Joseph, resembled his mother but had his father's blue eyes. Norris Wright, Stuart's fourth child, had the darkest complexion, with brown eyes and black hair.[19]

Cuney continued his liaison with Stuart throughout his second and third marriages. When he moved to Houston in 1853, leaving his plantation under the management of his overseer A. Livingston, Cuney took his slave family with him. Besides Stuart, his third wife, and his eleven black and white children in the same household, Philip Cuney's mother moved to Houston following the death of her second husband in 1854. Maud Cuney-Hare, in her biography of her father, Norris Wright, gives no indication of the treatment that Adeline received at the hands of her white grandmother, but the crowded household must have been stressful at times for all concerned. Stuart may have had more to deal with than her master's sexual exploitation. As historian John Blassingame points out, "white women were frequently infuriated by their husbands' infidelities in the quarters and took revenge on the black women involved." Since Stuart and her children lived in the same household, any actions taken against Stuart were probably subtle.[20]

Some writers before the 1970s echoed previous racially biased scholarship by putting the onus for sexual relationships on the slave instead of the master. Virginia Neale Hinze, for example, said that in this particular liaison: "Adeline was artful enough to keep it well established through her middle age and through two of Cuney's marriages. Her influence on him was such that by 1860 he had manumitted her and their seven children and educated their three sons." Hinze implies that Stuart manipulated Cuney to continue the sexual relationship for her benefit and that of their eight children. Yet Hinze ignores what historian Catherine Clinton calls the "sexual dynamics of southern race relations." According to Clinton: "Consent would never be more than a minor factor in a society where slaveowners maintained despotic rule. The female slave, for example, could not give herself freely, for she did not have herself to give: she already belonged to the master." Therefore, because of the nature of slavery, Stuart had no choice but to submit to the man who owned her.[21]

The Cuney family's move to Houston in 1853 became a turning point in the lives of Stuart and her children. Beginning then and continuing as his slave children grew into maturity, Cuney began to manumit and educate his mulatto offspring. Several reasons may account for his benevolence. His marriage to his third wife, Adeline Spurlock, the same year may have spurred him to ease household tensions. Or the move from the isolated countryside to an urban environment may have motivated Cuney to exhibit a more socially acceptable image. Most likely, Cuney had over the years developed a genuine fondness for Stuart and her children.

He arranged to send the boys to George B. Vashon's Wyle Street School for Colored Youth in Pittsburgh, Pennsylvania. The Wyle Street School was one of several institutions in Pittsburgh dedicated to teaching African American youth. As early as 1849, the city, together with local white churches and the African Methodist Episcopal church, began to fund independent black schools. Vashon conducted classes in the Wesleyan Church on Wyle Street. He charged a modest tuition and provided room and board for Nelson and Joseph Cuney, all paid for by their father. In 1858, Wyle Street had eighty-nine boys and sixty-nine girls attending. Philip Cuney freed Norris Wright at the age of thirteen, sending him to join his brothers in Pittsburgh.[22]

Cuney freed Stuart and her other children sometime following the manumission of Norris Wright in 1859. Jennie, one of Cuney's mulatto daughters who most resembled her father with his fair complexion, blue eyes, and blond hair, received special treatment. At considerable expense, Cuney sent Jennie to Madame Nichol's Institute for Young Ladies in Mannheim, Germany. Accompanying Jennie was another young woman with light features named Josephine Barbour. Upon their return Barbour married Joseph Cuney, while Jennie passed into the white community; Philip Cuney's reason for sending Jennie to Europe may have been for this purpose. Apparently, all contact with her immediate family ceased at that time. The other Cuney children obtained their educations in Freedmen Bureau schools following the war.[23]

Norris Wright Cuney

After a long illness, Philip Cuney died on January 8, 1866. Much remains unknown about him as a person. Politically, he left a competent if undistinguished legacy. Like many other planters, his way of life lay in ruins following the war. While his land holdings were extensive, Cuney's last will and testament described an estate burdened with debt. Perhaps his most important legacy became the manumission and education of his mulatto children. His actions in freeing and educating Norris Wright provided Texas with its most talented and successful African American politician of the nineteenth century. Philip Cuney's granddaughter, Maud Cuney-Hare, went on to become a talented and important figure among the early-twentieth-century black elite and left an impressive musical and literary legacy.

In many ways, Philip Cuney exemplified Williamson's slaveholding maverick. He went against the accepted but often abridged norms of southern society to pursue a relationship with his slave Adeline Stuart. He incorporated his children with her into his household while allowing Adeline a certain amount of independence regarding her other children. Later, Cuney openly violated the expectations of white society in Texas by first manumitting his slave children and then providing them with an education as they grew into maturity. He also took risks. Leaving the settled conditions of Louisiana, he moved west to start anew on the Texas frontier. Once there, he mortgaged his most important assets, his slaves, to pursue the often risky proposition of land speculation. In the Texas Senate, Cuney called for the resignation of a sitting federal judge of questionable ethics with no guarantee that the judge would vacate his position or would not seek retribution against his accuser in the future. Like some other slaveholders in the South, Philip Cuney took public risks, but he carried that attitude further to join a smaller group of mavericks who created interracial families.

CHAPTER 2

Norris Wright Cuney
Labor and Civic Leader

FOLLOWING THE CIVIL WAR, Norris Wright Cuney returned to Texas and settled in Galveston, a world away from the fertile farmland of Austin County but close to Houston, where as a youth he had lived for nine years. The beautiful island-port attracted many ambitious young black and white men. "Breezes fresh from the Gulf mingled with odors of oleander, and cape jasmine from the city gardens" counterbalanced the hustle and bustle of the fastest growing city in Texas. Under the protection of the Union Army, newly freed slaves joined a black presence in Galveston dating back to the time of Cabeza de Vaca. By 1870, over three thousand African Americans called Galveston home. During Reconstruction, the Freedmen's Bureau maintained its headquarters in Galveston, and the city became one of the bureau's real successes in Texas. The bureau provided protection and established schools for educating hundreds of illiterate freedmen. German families provided security and homes for northern teachers; Galveston served as the port of entry for hundreds of European immigrants, of whom many stayed, giving the city a cosmopolitan atmosphere. Cuney grew to love his new home and dedicated a large portion of his life to its success. He served as city alderman and organized African American dockworkers into a successful labor union.[1]

Wright Cuney also rose to leadership of the Republican Party and dominated the state organization until 1896, gaining friends and valuable alliances within the Republican National Committee. He obtained

appointment as collector of customs for Galveston, the most important post any African American would receive in the late-nineteenth-
century South. As a state party leader, he succeeded as no other black
politician, but nowhere did Cuney gain the respect of blacks and whites,
Democrats and Republicans, more than in his beloved Galveston.
Through his labor activities, he gained the respect of businessmen and
merchants while making possible the employment of hundreds of black
dockworkers. In his civic life he won election as a city alderman, became the commissioner of water works, and served on numerous boards
and commissions. Cuney received praise from city leaders for his personal honesty and integrity. No other black Galvestonian would be as
successful.

Cuney, as an urban black, seemed far removed from the mass of
nineteenth-century black Texans, who lived in rural areas pursuing agricultural endeavors in impoverished conditions. In many ways Cuney represented a new urban black middle class. As a mulatto he represented a
minority within a minority, though Cuney strongly identified himself as
a "Negro." Many men of mixed heritage within the first generation of
black leadership following the Civil War became members of a black
elite both culturally and politically. As the son of an upper-class white
man and a mulatto slave, Cuney represented an even more select group
of blacks who received an education and freedom from their white fathers. According to Joel Williamson, "It was almost as if mixing of this
special sort in late slavery had produced a new breed, preset to move into
the vanguard of their people when freedom came."[2]

White southerners, steeped in the ideology of slavery and black inferiority and feelings of guilt over miscegenation, refused to see a difference between mulattoes and darker-skinned blacks. Most southern states
codified this view into law. Some antebellum mulattoes, especially house
servants and others in close contact with their white fathers, often viewed
themselves as distinct from other blacks; but following the Civil War,
their interests fused with those of the black community. When freedmen
entered the political arena, they shared common enemies and objectives
that made this fusion permanent. Dark-skinned blacks viewed this relationship as positive. According to Williamson, "they needed verbal and
mathematical literacy, economic, political, and social education, and people
to teach their teachers." The mulatto elite along with northern mission-
aries provided that help.[3]

Mrs. Norris Wright Cuney

The extended Cuney family also made Galveston home. Joined by his brothers, Joseph and Nelson, and their mother, Adeline, Wright Cuney settled on Galveston's east side. All lived within a three-block radius of each other. Joseph, the eldest, later became an attorney, while Nelson became a building contractor. Wright, the budding politician, married sixteen-year-old Adelina Dowdie on July 5, 1871. Adelina, like her husband, was the progeny of a white planter and a mulatto slave. A woman of uncommon beauty, she appeared "small in figure, of fair complexion, with large grey eyes and curly black hair." Before her marriage, she obtained an education in bureau schools and planned on becoming a public schoolteacher. Besides advising and supporting her husband in his career,

Adelina became very active in church, charitable activities, and "in matters of social uplift." She possessed a "beautiful, dramatic soprano voice" and frequently sang in public.

Among "orange trees, plum and pomegranate, purple fig and mulberry trees," Cuney established a home for Adelina and his two children, Maud and Lloyd Garrison. Cuney went to great lengths to shelter his children from the often racist climate in which they lived. Although difficult, he did in many ways create what they remembered as an idyllic and happy home life for his family. Maud and Lloyd had seven cousins to play with, all living a few houses away, and the sandy beaches of the Gulf were within walking distance. Both parents put heavy emphasis on reading and education. According to Maud, "Christmas with the children's party and the candle-lighted tree, always brought us books galore." In the evenings Cuney read aloud the classics and poetry, especially Byron, to his children. Shakespeare became the central literary figure among the extended household. The cousins would memorize long passages of his plays, and Shakespearean performances became a common event.[4]

Adelina Cuney ran the household, tending to the religion of the family and the discipline of the children. Wright belonged to no church but provided through his example guidance for his children. As a doting father, he found it difficult to withstand the "tears and pleading" of his children. Cuney nevertheless taught them self-control, reminding them often to "do as you please, but please do right." He instilled in his children a deep sense of racial pride and a "hatred" for any form of racism or racial accommodation. A lifelong insomniac, Cuney substituted work for sleep but still made time for family discussions and readings after dinner, accompanied by wine and the fine cigars he smoked incessantly.[5]

The excitement and growth of Galveston sometimes overshadowed the problems that it shared with most nineteenth-century cities. Galveston had a high mortality rate, in part because it lacked proper sanitation facilities and trash removal, which led to a variety of ills such as typhoid, dysentery, and consumption. As a semitropical island and port city, Galveston had no shortage of mosquitoes and thus no shortage of yellow fever. One of the worst epidemics occurred in 1867 shortly after Cuney's return. Blacks generally succumbed to yellow fever in fewer numbers and suffered less severely from the illness than whites. When thousands of whites contracted the fever, blacks stepped in as nurses and caregivers.

Cuney became one of many African Americans who nursed white Galvestonians in their time of need. While he too came down with the fever, he made a quick recovery. Over eighteen hundred people died.[6]

Unselfish care given by African Americans in the epidemic was apparently a short-lived memory for many whites, who during Reconstruction became antagonistic over black voting rights and citizenship in Galveston. Most whites also resented the strong federal presence in their town and especially disliked the influx of black immigrants. The city established strong vagrancy laws to imprison homeless freedmen. Whites complained of drunken freedmen roaming the streets, though the abundance of saloons probably resulted in many more drunken whites. Whites showed little concern for the immense difficulties faced by the newly freed slaves. To Galveston's credit, though, whites did not carry out such violent retribution against freedmen as often took place in other parts of Texas.[7]

Only nineteen when he moved to Galveston, Wright Cuney certainly did not view himself as a member of the black elite. Surviving from one day to next became his main concern. What he did from the time of his arrival to his first position of record in 1870 is unknown. The extended family, which remained close throughout the late nineteenth century, no doubt relied upon each other for moral and financial support. Cuney may have worked with his older brother, Nelson, a local painting contractor. The fact that the three Cuney brothers were literate gave them an advantage over most blacks in the job market. By the early 1870s, Cuney had established himself in the black community as president of the Union League. By 1871, he began to attract the notice of whites.

Major changes took place for blacks during Reconstruction and afterward. Many African Americans who moved from rural settings to the cities formed large separate black enclaves. Because of white prejudice and a desire to exert their independence from whites, black Texans organized their own churches, schools, and social organizations. For the vast majority of African Americans, the church became the focal point of their lives. There blacks had complete control. The church played an important role in the lives of Adelina and the Cuney children. Later their son, Lloyd, became an official in the Congregationalist church. While Wright Cuney did not actively participate in the church along with his wife and family, he did become heavily involved in Masonic activity.[8]

Next to the church, such fraternal organizations in many communities provided the most important social contact for black males. Cuney gained initiation into Prince Hall Freemasonry on July 24, 1874. Prince Hall, the oldest and most respected black fraternity, originated in Boston, Massachusetts, in 1775. Hall and fifteen others, all free blacks, received initiation into a lodge of the British army. Following the American Revolution, he tried and failed to obtain a charter for a Masonic lodge from Massachusetts. Because of white opposition, Hall instead obtained a charter from the Grand Lodge of London in 1784. The fraternity quickly spread throughout North America, including seven southern states by 1869. In 1872 the Grand Lodge of Kansas chartered three Texas lodges, including one in Galveston. On August 19, 1875, black Masons organized the Grand Lodge of Texas and elected Cuney as grand master. Within five years the fraternity had spread throughout the state, accumulating property valued over $150,000.[9]

The establishment of black lodges in Texas caused white Masons great discomfort. Just as in other southern states, white Masons in Texas refused to recognize black Masonic legitimacy. While assisting in ceremonies marking the 100th anniversary Prince Hall meeting in June, 1875, in Boston, Cuney joined others in demonstrating against whites who refused to recognize blacks as Masons. Foreign Masonic lodges, including orders in England and Germany, publicly recognized black legitimacy and called upon white Americans to do the same. After this, some white northern lodges, including the largest, the Grand Lodge of Ohio, recognized their black brothers. Southern fraternities refused recognition until the mid–twentieth century.[10]

As Grand Master Cuney gained valuable leadership experience, he also gained a valuable network of friends and supporters not only in Texas but also throughout the nation. Grand lodges in their particular states are semi-independent organizations invested with legislative and judicial functions. Cuney, as chief executive officer, set the stage for an amazing growth of black Masonic activity in the Lone Star State. By the mid-1870s, Cuney had gained a statewide reputation as an up-and-coming black leader.[11]

Galveston's civic and community leaders began to take notice of the fraternal leader and Republican politician. Promotion-minded businessmen, merchants, and civic leaders wanted to make Galveston the leading Gulf port, hoping to surpass New Orleans in cotton and grain shipments. To do this they needed better levies, a deeper harbor, and a plan for both municipal growth and city government that would attract outside investment. Civic leaders reorganized the Galveston Chamber of Commerce to promote harbor improvements.[12]

A key figure in developing the city's forward-looking ideas became William L. Moody, founder of one of the wealthiest families in Texas. Born in Virginia, Moody moved to the state following the Civil War. During the conflict he had received several decorations for bravery and achieved the rank of colonel. In 1872 he helped organize the Galveston Cotton Exchange and the Colorado and Santa Fe Railway. A partisan Democrat, he nevertheless sought the cooperation and advice of Galveston's black leadership in his plans. When Moody and other white leaders called for a meeting of city leaders at the Cotton Exchange to begin harbor improvements, they asked Cuney to participate.[13]

Cuney made his first try for city office in 1875. Even with Reconstruction at an end and Edmund Davis no longer governor, Republicans felt they still had enough strength in Galveston to win the mayoral election. Cuney ran a conservative campaign based on issues of education and economic growth. In an era of increasing hostility toward blacks, Cuney's Democratic opponent, Robert Fulton, did not use race as an issue. With a solid Democrat majority in Galveston, he may have thought it not necessary, or more likely, Fulton wanted to project a positive image of his city to outsiders. Fulton easily won. Instead of antagonizing white businessmen and merchants, Cuney's issue-oriented and conservative campaign gained him their respect. Following the election, Fulton praised Cuney for "his excellent qualities as a public man."[14]

Leadership by Cuney during business-labor troubles in 1877 gained him additional respect and notice within the white and black communities. For days prior to July 30 of that year, rumors spread through Galveston that black workers were about to strike. No particular union planned the walkout, and little labor organizing took place, but Monday morning in front of the Garirdin Building, a group of fifty black men began urging workers in the vicinity to strike. Others quickly joined in as the group began marching down the Strand, collecting additional support as they moved toward the courthouse.

Many strikers came from the Narrow Gauge Railroad Company, laying down track. Black workers also came from the Galveston Flour Mill, from the construction site of the new St. Patrick's Catholic Church, and areas all over the city. Many black women also left their domestic jobs to participate. The deputy chief of police and a detachment of officers followed the strikers close behind. At one point, the mayor stopped the march, warning participants that "they were in a fair way to becoming violators of the public peace which it was his duty to protect, and he would do it at all hazards." Undeterred, they continued collecting more workers as they marched.[15]

The first day of the strike ended with several speeches and a meeting conducted by a white Irish immigrant, Michael Burns. The strikers passed resolutions criticizing employers who reduced wages and demanding a raise in pay from an average of $1.50 to $2.00 a day. Tensions rose the following day with news that police had wounded a black man named Beauregard and arrested several strikers. Following these incidents, other whites met at Artillery Hall and formed several "citizen-soldier" companies. Strikers began to notice a marked increase of whites carrying guns.

That afternoon a more formal meeting took place, again led by Burns. A series of committees, formed the previous night, continued to negotiate with employers. Burns urged the strikers to go home peacefully and return at 7:00 that evening to hear the committee reports. He warned that "soldiers had been engaged all day with guns on their shoulders." Some strikers wanted a confrontation. One yelled out, "D——d their guns! We can whip them and their guns too, soon enough when we start for them." Order prevailed, however, as the meeting adjourned.[16]

That evening the committees reported only limited success. The Narrow Gauge Railroad promised a pay raise, but only if strikers returned to work immediately. Burns suggested that they hold out for five or six weeks, and by that time the "cars and locomotives would run off the track and occasion a greater amount of loss to the railroad owners than raising the price of wages." Several wanted the policemen who shot "the innocent colored man arrested." Some called for retribution. Then many in the crowd began to call for Wright Cuney to speak.

When he addressed the crowd, Cuney denigrated those who called for violence, which would only lead to "the destruction of their own best interests." He warned them that there "were over 700 armed men—trained soldiers—in the city, who could annihilate them in an hour," and if they could not, "a 1,000 men under arms" from Houston would finish the job. Cuney criticized the strikers for "creating all sorts of discord, and stirring up all sorts of bad blood." He condemned "the follies into which the colored men had fallen" and pointed out that less than 300 blacks out of a labor force of 1,500 had joined the strike. If they continued their strike, then "every good citizen would be found on the side of law . . . and the strikers would be the sufferers in the end for the foolishness of which they had already been guilty in a vain attempt to revolutionize the industrial interests of the city." He told the strikers to go home and on the "morrow find work at any price." The *Galveston Daily News* strongly opposed the strike, so its editors may have reported only the aspects of Cuney's speech that reflected that opposition, but throughout his political career, Cuney identified himself with a Republican ideology that may have influenced his opposition to the strike. After Cuney's speech, the strike began to dissolve despite the pleas of the more radical workers to continue.[17]

After this, few doubted Cuney's leadership position within the Galveston black community. City leaders appreciated his efforts in diffusing a dangerous situation and preventing possible harm to Galveston's reputation. A practical man, Cuney knew the dangers members of the black minority faced at the hands of a racially biased society when they challenged the status quo. At the same time, he had complete faith in the American system and optimistically believed African Americans could prevail if they worked within that system. But doing so for Cuney did not preclude leading and even manipulating the system toward a more favorable outcome. For the next ten years, Cuney would turn black labor weakness into a strength, pitting one group of whites against another to gain a permanent position for black screwmen on Galveston's docks.

The white Screwmen's Benevolent Association (SBA) represented the most powerful union on Galveston's docks during the 1870s and 1880s. Formed in 1866, the union held a virtual monopoly in its field. By using brute strength and screwjacks, skilled screwmen could stow and pack 15–20 percent more cotton in a ship than would otherwise be possible. They could determine whether or not a cotton shipper would be profitable. Their skill and limited numbers gave them increased leverage over shippers. The union used its monopoly to great advantage. Wages and benefits for its membership were some of the highest in Texas. Members received sickness and death benefits and became part of a tight-knit social group. The most influential members were contracting stevedores who managed individual screwmen gangs. Rules required that only official members could load ships, and an 1869 SBA resolution precluded blacks from becoming members.[18]

The all-white screwmen's union wanted to keep blacks out at all costs. In 1879, apparently on Cuney's advice, black longshoremen organized the Cotton Jammer's Association with the expressed aim of obtaining screwmen contracts. SBA members reacted quickly by establishing a special committee to investigate the new organization and to keep blacks off the ships. Through SBA influence, no blacks obtained screwmen positions. Eventually, the SBA overplayed its hand. In 1880 the association limited to seventy-five single bales the amount of cotton any one member could load in one day's work; anyone who loaded more would be fined. Two years later, in an apparent show of strength and solidarity, the SBA called a "work holiday" without explanation.

By 1883, increasing cotton exports together with reduced workloads began to cause labor shortages during peak periods. Cuney saw an opportunity for black screwmen. Out of his own pocket, he purchased $2,500 worth of tools and organized the Screwmen's Benevolent Association (No. 2). He then sent a letter to Colonel Moody, president of the Cotton Exchange: "Having observed that the commercial importance of Galveston has been in a measure jeopardized by the insufficiency of skilled labor necessary in loading seagoing vessels with cotton and having reason to believe that accessions to that class of labor through present channels will not be large enough to meet the demands of our growing commerce for another season, I have thought it proper to call your attention to the fact that there are a large number of laborers admirably adapted by the character of their pursuits to supply this necessity. I allude to the colored men who now have a scanty livelihood by hard labor along the shore."[19]

Moody and the Cotton Exchange wrote Cuney back the next day "heartily" welcoming the new labor force. The exchange's action cleared the way for Cuney to seek contracts for black screwmen. Shippers, tired of the white SBA's attitude and work slowdowns, did not flinch from hiring blacks. In his new position as a contracting stevedore and president of the union, Cuney obtained for black screwmen their first job loading the ship *Albion* on Morgan's Wharf. On April 2, 1883, these men showed up for work under the protection of Galveston police. Whites immediately went on strike. Shortly afterward, Captain Sawyer of the Mallory Steamship Line contacted Cuney offering another contract to replace striking screwmen on the New York dock. Cuney agreed but asked for and secured guarantees that blacks would henceforth receive an equal opportunity for future employment and would not be used as "catspaws to pull the chestnuts out of the fire." In a speech before the black screwmen, he expressed the desire of the union to cooperate with their white counterparts. Cuney said he was only seeking justice for African American workers and asked "whether the colored man should not be given a fair chance with others in the struggle for bread."[20]

What seemed impossible just a short time before became a reality as black screwmen began to work loading ships. Cuney knew white screwmen would strike rather than share the abundance of work even they could not perform. Members of the Cotton Exchange unanimously passed a resolution critical of the white SBA, calling the exclusion of black screwmen "unreasonable and detrimental to the best interest of this Port." Exchange members appropriated ten thousand dollars to "protect commerce." The white SBA bought newspaper space at other southern ports alerting them of the strike. The white union accused shippers of seeking retribution for the SBA's high wages and job control. From New Orleans, Mobile, and the Knights of Labor came letters of sympathy for the white workers. The union members at Mobile offered the white screwmen of Galveston the right to work at their docks. New Orleans screwmen's union called blacks usurpers and passed a resolution to "do all in its power to aid and assist our Brother Screwmen of Galveston."[21]

On May 11 the SBA voted to require that all white screwmen become members before they could work on the Galveston wharfs. Tensions on both sides rose as rumors spread of possible violence directed against Cuney. That evening, black screwmen kept vigil around his home. Cuney pleaded with his wife to take the children to his brother's house for protection, but she refused and took up a position at the backdoor, looking for possible attackers. Well-armed friends and neighbors joined the screwmen protecting their leader. City police also kept watch over the area. Probably because of the overwhelming force protecting Cuney, no violence occurred.[22]

When the strike continued into the summer, white militancy seemed to diminish in the face of opposition from shippers, merchants, and civic leaders. In June the white SBA members planned an annual picnic and dance, their most important social occasion. This year they pledged not to hire any "Negro band." To add insult to injury, no white entertainment could be found, forcing the union to hire a black band anyway, as Cuney brought in black screwmen from New Orleans to facilitate the increasing workload.[23]

As the busy fall season approached, the strikers' situation became more tenuous as Cuney continued to supply workers. Members of the Cotton Exchange did not relent in their opposition. Divisions within the white SBA began to develop, and the union held several heated meetings. Then on August 27, the membership voted seventy-nine to seventy-two to go back to work unconditionally. Cuney and the black screwmen won the day. The white SBA continued as a powerful union, but skilled black screwmen now worked on Galveston's docks and would continue to do so. In the process Cuney created a working relationship with Galveston's largest shipper, the Mallory Steamship Line. In 1885, white screwmen proposed a division of labor, with "the white and colored laborers working week in and week out upon the basis of two steamers to the week." Cuney and the black SBA rejected the idea, refusing to "dictate to Captain Sawyer, agent of the Mallory Line, whom he shall employ, or map out for him any division of labor." Because Sawyer and other shippers continued to uphold their pledges to the black SBA, Cuney felt honor-bound not to cooperate with white screwmen. When the Knights of Labor struck the Mallory Steamship Line in 1885, Cuney's organization of black screwmen and other black longshoremen helped Mallory defeat the strike.[24]

The involvement of Cuney in the labor troubles of 1877 and in the creation of a black SBA revolved around the protection and promotion of black labor. He did not pursue labor organization in the traditional sense and did not act as a traditional labor boss. Even though the Knights of Labor allowed blacks to join its ranks, albeit in separate locals, he did not foresee blacks becoming an important part of a southern labor movement that whites dominated. According to Cuney, "with the growth of the labor union the black man has been crowded out." He wanted blacks to fight back against white labor domination and used the white unions' racial attitudes to the black man's advantage. Cuney may have felt that only black leadership would act in the own best interest of other African Americans.[25]

Cuney's attitude toward white labor reflected the developing view held by many members of the black elite in the late nineteenth and early twentieth centuries. Many of those in leadership positions became antagonistic toward white unionism because of its antiblack bias and violence directed against black strikebreakers. According to Kevin Gaines, "black middle-class identity was often defined in relation to the racial prejudice of working-class whites." Like Cuney, other black leaders acted for black laborers by appealing to "profit seeking capitalists for economic salvation." Nativism may also have played a part. Black elites and their white counterparts often "associated unions and radicalism with foreign born workers." In Galveston the majority of white screwmen were recent immigrants. While Cuney did not publicly make this an issue, it may in part account for his alliance with white businessmen.[26]

Cuney saw industrial education as one way for African Americans to fight back against the dominance of skilled white labor. Just like many young whites, Cuney argued, young blacks were also "born with the soul of invention and the deftness of a machinist" and should make the most of it. If African Americans could then use that skill in the middle of a strike, they could prove to employers they could do the job as well as any white man. In a commencement address at Paul Quinn College in Waco, Cuney strongly supported black intellectual training and also spoke of the urgent need for industrial education:

> Progressive national life means progressive industrial life. The one is dependent upon the success of the other. And that race which employs the energy and thrift, is the one which quickly realizes the meaning of the term.
>
> As it is with other members of the human family it must be with us. If we would succeed in life and place ourselves above a plane of continual helplessness we must foster a spirit of industrial as well as intellectual life. In other words we must teach our boys and girls mechanical trades; encourage commercial undertakings and recognize manly and womanly capabilities. Thirty years of freedom have demonstrated that the colored man has a high degree of mechanical genius; that he can take his place, when properly trained, in the ranks of the skilled labor of the world, and there hold his own.[27]

Although he never specifically mentioned the idea as a concept, Cuney's address outlined a self-help approach to black economic problems. He believed the experience on the wharves of Galveston proved his argument. Skilled black laborers demonstrated they were equal, if not better than, their white counterparts. White employers lavished high praise and recognition on black screwmen. Thomas England, owner of the steamship *Jane,* for example, noted that Cuney's crew loaded thirty-five thousand pounds more cotton in his ship than white screwmen did in New Orleans. Nine other Galveston shippers, including Captain Sawyer of Mallory Steamship Line, acknowledged the larger shiploads, praising black screwmen and recommending them to other shippers.[28]

In 1883, after citywide recognition of his labor victory, Cuney decided to try again for municipal office. He announced for alderman of the Twelfth Ward, in which whites outnumbered blacks 1,445 to 1,089. Much had changed since his failed mayoral candidacy of 1875. As in many cities across the nation, Galveston politics began to pursue, as much as possible, a nonpartisan approach. Neither major party offered its own candidates for public office but instead supported independent city parties of the "People's ticket" and "Citizen's ticket." Cuney ran on the Citizen's ticket. While a nonpartisan approach aided Galveston's leading Republican in gaining office, the electoral opportunities for African Americans in a city with an overwhelming white majority appeared small. Cuney became the exception. He had widespread name recognition. His labor activities gained the recognition and respect of powerful economic interests in the city, prompting the *Galveston Daily News* to praise Cuney for his "wise and conservative" policies.[29]

The same conservatism praised by the *Daily News* created strong anti-Cuney feelings from white labor. They accused him of collusion with business interests in depriving "white men of bread and meat." Far from harming the Cuney candidacy, union attacks only increased his support among many black and white citizens. He also formed an alliance with mayoral candidate R. L. Fulton, convincing many within the Republican Party to support the ex-Confederate and Democrat. With white voters outnumbering blacks, Cuney won the election by a slim twenty-four-vote margin.[30]

The *Daily News* correctly identified Cuney's philosophy of government regarding city affairs. The new alderman believed the city should operate as a "corporation and every citizen is a stock holder to the extent of his vote and the dividend this people ought to demand from those who are entrusted with the conduct of their business, is an honest and economical administration of government, courage in the assessment and collection of revenues, and an honest and faithful expenditure, with a view to giving as many public improvements as possible after paying the necessary running expenses." He would vote time and again for efficiency in government and against what he considered unneeded expenses, especially in adding personnel to the city bureaucracy. At the same time, he usually supported improvements to city streets, harbors, waterworks, education, and anything else that might contribute to future growth as long as it did not entail new taxes. He took a special interest in improved living conditions within the black community, pursuing those interests no matter what the political costs. One such occasion involved the creation of Ball High School.[31]

Wealthy Galvestonian George Ball bequeathed fifty thousand dollars to the city for construction of a new high school "permanently dedicated to free public schools." The council voted unanimously to accept the donation. After completion of the school, Cuney presented a motion to integrate the school, which the council approved. Claiming Ball only wanted the school segregated, his heirs immediately offered ten thousand dollars more if the city guaranteed the school would only be for white students. Cuney found the idea repugnant and contrary to a government that is supposed to know "no race distinction." The transparent bribe worked, for the white aldermen on the council voted to reconsider Cuney's motion. Cuney spoke passionately, asking not for "social equality" but for justice and "educational advantages for colored people, particularly in systems of public education, that were equal and free of prejudice." After losing the vote, Cuney called a special meeting of the Republican County Executive Committee to pledge party support for candidates who promised to oppose those not committed to "colored children's equal rights." When the white chairman of the committee opposed the pledge, Cuney forced him to resign. Afterward, the school board voted to create a black high school equal to the white school, and Cuney rescinded his pledge.[32]

Despite council decisions like Ball's donation, Cuney and Mayor Fulton became good friends. Fulton, a former secessionist and captain in the Confederate Army, saw himself as a southern progressive and an adherent of Henry Grady's "New South." He wanted to project a positive image of Galveston with "good will, peace, progress, reconciliation and equal rights to all." While many of his actions failed to live up to his rhetoric, Fulton reached out to Galveston's black community through Cuney. Campaign gatherings in Galveston, as in other cities during the nineteenth century, served not only as political but also as social events. Fulton, in his five campaigns for mayor, became the only white candidate actively to seek black support by providing picnics, barbecues, and other entertainment. Through his efforts and the support of Cuney, Fulton garnered the lion's share of black electoral support.[33]

As an alderman, Cuney served on many different committees. While he worked diligently on all his assignments, Cuney took special interest in the Committees on Streets and Alleys, Claims and Accounts, and Waterworks. All three reflected the priorities of his governmental philosophy. Through claims and accounts, he sought to end corruption, promote efficiency, and contractor accountability. With aldermen from twelve different wards, many of whom served as committee chairmen, corruption became an ongoing problem. Coziness often developed between the committee members and contractors; contracts sometimes went to friends and relatives instead of the lowest bidder. Throughout his career, Cuney took a dim view of such practices, which brought him high praise for his honesty and integrity.

When Alderman Frank Mitchell, chairman of the Committee on Streets and Alleys, paid 12.5 cents for shell used in paving instead of the going rate of 0.10 cents, Cuney smelled a rat and investigated. He charged the committee with corruption after finding that not only did the city pay too much but also paid for 1,745 pounds more than they received. Further, his investigation showed that the contractor was an employee of the city engineer. Apparently seeing little wrongdoing, the council only sanctioned Mitchell for "loose duty." Cuney influenced the mayor to appoint a special reform committee that proposed amending the city charter to make such practices illegal.[34]

Cuney's actions, though laudable, had a negative outcome. Other aldermen apparently felt quite comfortable with corruption and made Cuney pay for upsetting the applecart. He served with three aldermen and three citizens on the Charter Committee established by the mayor but found himself in the minority time and again during deliberations. In a transparent move to end the influence of Cuney and black voters on the council, committee members voted to change the way aldermen obtained election. In a five-to-one vote, they proposed election of aldermen by the entire city rather than by individual wards, which if adopted would effectively eliminate black representation. Cuney countered with a proposal before the council as a whole that would instead elect six aldermen by wards, including the Twelfth, and six from the city at large. After a heated debate, the council voted against even considering the Cuney motion. He again tried to enact this reform before the state legislature but without success. Such citywide voting, however, apparently fit well into the objectives of many legislators during the 1880s and 1890s to disfranchise black voters.[35]

Most of Cuney's work on the council resulted in positive and constructive outcomes. Cuney sought to improve Galveston's water, a problem plaguing the city throughout much of the nineteenth century. Because of the vast expense, past city councils refused to build a modern waterworks that would provide an efficient water supply. In the city election of 1885, Cuney and several other candidates campaigned for a new facility. In late 1884 the council had voted, over Fulton's veto, for its construction.

Without the mayor's cooperation, the project never got off the ground, at least not until after the "Great Fire" of 1885. On a windy day in November, a fire broke out at the city ironworks at 17th Street and the Strand and spread quickly. For five hours a raging inferno consumed forty-two blocks and 568 homes and businesses. Fire hydrants that pumped seawater proved woefully inadequate for the job. Water pressure was almost nonexistent and several hydrants became clogged with sea shells.[36]

Mayor Fulton saw the folly of his intransigence and called a special council meeting to deal with the crisis. Cuney and the other aldermen voted to appropriate funds to repair city infrastructure destroyed by the fire. To deal with the water crisis, the mayor appointed Cuney and two other aldermen as a committee to find alternatives for Galveston's water supply. They recommended charter amendments calling for construction of a modern facility, and on Cuney's motion the council adopted the report. When Cuney left office in 1887, Fulton appointed him to a two-year term as waterworks commissioner. Cuney played an integral part in overseeing the project. By 1889, after the city spent $450,000, a new and modern waterworks began operation with seventeen thousand feet of water mains supplying two million gallons of water.[37]

In 1885 Cuney announced for reelection. His enemies hoped the new city-at-large electoral process would eliminate him from the council. Just to make sure he lost, his opponents stuffed ballot boxes and destroyed ballots in several wards. The initial vote count showed him losing by 135 votes. Cuney contested the outcome. A subsequent investigation established that fraud did take place. In the Eleventh Ward, where he received only twenty-one votes, ninety-seven citizens testified as voting for Cuney, including A. H. Willie, chief justice of the Texas Supreme Court. Overall, the council found over three hundred destroyed or substituted ballots and swore Cuney into office. Fulton also won reelection as mayor.[38]

In his second term, Cuney became involved in another controversy over modernizing the city. New inventions interested him. One such device, the telephone, came to Galveston in the late 1870s, and a Galveston-to-Houston telephone exchange began service in 1881. Cuney was one of the first to use the telephone in 1881 to talk to a fellow Republican in Houston. Another invention that Cuney took an interest in, the electric light, had possibilities for improving downtown Galveston. He became impressed with electric lights in 1882, when Brush Electric Company opened for business and lit up 26th Street. When the council decided the time had come to light city streets, a debate took place on how best to do it. Cuney favored the use of archlights and proposed that method to the council. But the local gas company, an old and prominent business, had many friends on the council, which opted for gas lighting.[39]

Mayor Fulton sided with Cuney, not because he favored electric lights but because he believed the gas company charged too much. He vetoed the contract only to have his veto overridden. Cuney thus had added another powerful enemy to an already long list. Fulton had enemies too, though without the additional burden of being black. In the next election, opponents drew what the *Daily News* called the "color line." The gas company, other special interests, and old-line city politicians made Cuney a special target. On the Citizen's ticket, William K. McAlpine obtained the mayoral nomination. President of the school board of trustees, McAlpine supported segregation of city schools and had a great dislike for "Cuney that interfering Negro." His strategy was to make race the main issue, linking Fulton and Cuney together. He urged voters to support the entire Citizen's ticket except for Cuney, whom they sacrificed in support of his opponent on the People's ticket, C. J. Allen.[40]

In a contentious campaign, the opponents of Fulton and Cuney accused the mayor of being Cuney's puppet and the "colored man's candidate." Race had been an issue in previous elections, but in the past the opposition never made it the only issue. In such an environment, Cuney lost much of his white support. On election day, whites kept blacks from voting in several wards, especially in the Sixth, where violence took place. With black support and the votes of the white majority, Fulton won reelection, but for Cuney time had run out. While they overwhelmingly voted for Cuney, African Americans did not have the numbers to overcome the new at-large electoral system. After his defeat, the *Daily News* called Cuney "an excellent alderman . . . downed by race prejudice."[41]

Cuney took his alderman responsibilities very seriously. He saw city politics as nonpartisan. Only once, during debate over integrating Ball High School, an issue of great political and social significance for African Americans, did Cuney merge city politics with the Republican Party. White aldermen who served with Cuney respected his abilities and honesty, a repeated observation regarding him throughout his career. Many of his duties on the council revolved around the problems of individual citizens and everyday city business, but on important issues like water, education, and corruption, Cuney did not shy away from controversy. He represented no special interest except his dedication to "his people" and to Galveston. His alderman career ended only after his enemies united and made his race the main issue.

The manipulation of voting districts to eliminate African American representation in government represented only one form of white racism confronting black Texans. During the 1880s and 1890s, African Americans faced a new form through the establishment of "Jim Crow" laws. Throughout his busy life, Cuney maintained a dedication to black civil rights. Just as he believed in solving black labor problems within the political system, he thought infringements of black civil rights should find redress through the courts. From theaters to train cars, African Americans protested time and again when victimized by racist or unequal treatment. Galveston blacks, especially women, had a long and admirable history of defiance and protest. Even before the passage of separate-coach laws, blacks often faced exclusion from train cars. Adelina Cuney, on her way to meet Wright at a political meeting in Houston, had the doors to her first-class train car locked in front of her. Refusing to let that stand, she asked her brother-in-law, Joseph, to hoist her through an open window and then took her seat.[42]

Individual acts of defiance in Galveston often led to group or mass protests, usually with Cuney as spokesman and leader. In late 1875 Henry Greenwall, manager of the Tremont Opera House in Galveston, refused a black woman, Mary Miller, the seat for which she had paid. She sued under the new Civil Rights Act of 1875. The act, introduced by Sen. Charles Sumner, a longtime advocate of black civil rights, included stiff penalties for "denying any citizen full and equal enjoyment of inns, public conveyances, theaters, and other places of public amusement." The Miller case went before U.S. District Judge Amos Morrill. Though he disliked the new law and the case before him, Judge Morrill had no alternative but to find Greenwall guilty and fine him five hundred dollars. The judge publicly stated that "he wished the fine could be one cent." Morrill allowed Greenwall to leave without bond, then inexplicably dismissed the fine several days later.

Outraged blacks, under the leadership of Cuney, called a mass meeting to protest. Reverend Randolph, a black Methodist minister in whose church the packed meeting took place, told those present, "it was better that a people perish in a day than live in disgrace." Cuney gave an angry and impassioned speech against Judge Morrill and his decision to drop the fine. He exposed the double standard of justice for blacks in the court system. He described his own experience of receiving a heavy fine for forgetting to pay a cigar license and argued that any black man would go to prison for what Greenwall did. Cuney went on to say: "Greenwall violated the right of an individual and the court rights of the colored people, upon whom rest the heel of oppression, and whose immunities guaranteed by the law are sought to be withheld from them. I boldly affirm that Judge Morrill is unfit to occupy a place on the bench. Your presence, fellow citizens, encourages me to advance boldly in a matter in which we, the colored race, are interested. We must speak out when the occasion demands it, for by silence we invite oppression." Greenwall continued as theater manager and continued to segregate by race. Cuney, as a matter of principle, refused to frequent southern theaters not owned by African Americans.[43]

The U.S. Supreme Court ruled the Civil Rights Act unconstitutional in 1883. By the mid-1880s, segregation of public accommodations and schools in Texas became a matter of fact. Whites could assuage their consciences by supporting the idea of separate but equal. Nothing exposed white hypocrisy more than separate train cars. The Texas legislature allowed railroads to "require" separate coaches in 1889 and made it mandatory two years later. Cuney, who doubted whites really wanted separate coaches, saw the law more as a blatant appeal to prejudice. He wrote to a friend:

I think it an undeniable fact that if there was any great public demand for separate cars in this state, the Railroad would put them on obedient to the demand and I can assure you that it would be far more desirable to be wronged by a railroad corporation than by the state, which I ought to and want to love.

Hundreds, perhaps, of white and colored people transact business on the cars going from place to place, but under this bill they will be denied this privilege. Look at the bill in any light you may, one is forced to the conclusion that it is uncalled for, unwise, a violation of the rights of property, and a brutal invasion of the rights of a people whose consciences will feel keenly the wrong done them by the New South in its effort to reverse fate and check the growth of a broader and better humanity.

In September of that year, under Cuney's guidance, a state "colored men's convention" passed resolutions opposing the new law.[44]

Cuney not only urged others to fight back against segregation but also reserved the right to challenge the law himself. In 1892, ill and on his way to a health spa in Hot Springs, Arkansas, for rest and recuperation, Cuney bought his usual first-class ticket on the Great Northern Pacific Railroad. When he went to purchase his accommodations in a Pullman Palace sleeping car. Under orders from the company, the agent refused to sell accommodations to the collector of customs and leader of the Texas Republican Party, a friend of powerful national leaders. Then the conductor refused his first-class seating. With the second-class and baggage cars full, Cuney "had to sit on the brake wheel part of the time," obviously a very separate and unequal accommodation. Cuney sued Pullman Palace Car Company for five thousand dollars in physical and mental damages.

In a Galveston trial before an all-white jury, Pullman and Great Northern testimony reflected contradictory policies. The railroad reiterated its "whites only" first-class-ticket policy but had no explanation for why it sold Cuney a first-class ticket. Pullman company representatives testified it was not their policy to exclude blacks from sleeping cars, but they did at times defer to the railroad. In cross-examination, the Pullman representative acknowledged, "I am employed by the Pullman palace car company; I work for Mr. Pullman and the Pullman car company only." While he violated the policy of his own company regarding blacks, he did not violate the railroad policy. Jury members spent less than thirty minutes before finding in favor of the Pullman Company. Cuney appealed the decision, though with similar results.[45]

Cuney's enemies may have colluded to embarrass the Republican leader. A frequent traveler, well known to Pullman and railroad officials, Cuney became an attractive target on whom to test the new law. In refusing such a powerful African American his first-class accommodations, they sent a clear message to other blacks. Many whites may have found pleasure in the embarrassment dealt such an important black leader. For Cuney and others, it only strengthened their resolve to protest such injustices; black Texans continued to resist civil rights violations.

While segregated train cars became a fact in the late nineteenth century, segregation in education had become a reality during Reconstruction. Thus, the battle in education became a fight for at least a semblance of equal facilities. For Cuney, African American education and creation of eleemosynary institutions for blacks became a consistent theme. He became deeply involved in education beginning in 1871, when Gov. Edmund Davis appointed him to the newly formed Galveston School Board. In 1868 E. M. Wheelock, former head of Freedmen's Bureau schools in Texas, developed a plan for creating public schools headed by a state board of education and dividing Texas into school districts controlled by local school boards. Under the Wheelock plan, adopted by the Twelfth Legislature, decisions concerning segregated facilities were left to local school boards. Galveston, like other districts, opted for segregated schools.[46]

Public education, as established during Reconstruction, became an important target of whites for change. The Texas Constitution of 1875 ended Wheelock's forward-looking plan for schools. Besides requiring segregation by law, the constitution ended state control of public education, leaving schools entirely in the hands of local officials. Almost immediately black education began to suffer. Although providing limited operating expenses, the constitution provided no tax base necessary for buildings and equipment. Whites who controlled local education provided little for their own children and even less for blacks. In his failed 1875 campaign for the legislature, Cuney had presented a very progressive school proposal similar to ideas finally adopted in the twentieth century. He proposed a nine-month school term, setting "scholastic age from 7 to 18 years," and "levying a specific tax" for public education.[47]

Cuney disliked segregation but saw no alternative, especially because of white opposition to black education. Besides whites' belief in black inferiority, they also feared that African Americans sought social equal-

ity. To such fears, Cuney responded that he did not ask for "social equality for my race. That is a matter no law can touch. . . . But in matters of
education and state charity there certainly should be no distinction." Since
segregated schools and charitable institutions were a matter of fact, Cuney
fought to make black institutions equal to those of whites.[48]

Largely because of these efforts, Galveston provided better schools
for blacks than most other Texas cities. Cuney in 1881 used his own funds
and donations from white Galvestonians to open a black kindergarten
in St. Paul's Methodist Church. He served on its advisory board until
his death in 1897. For black students who could not attend school during
the day and for adults who wanted an education, Cuney convinced school
trustees in 1884 to create three different night schools. Following the
Ball High School controversy, Cuney received concessions from school
board trustees leading to the establishment of Central High School for
blacks in 1885. His daughter, Maud, attended Central and was among
the first class of graduates. At her graduation ceremonies she performed
a piano recital and read a "well received" essay entitled "Necessity of a
High School Education." Central High became an integral part of the
Galveston African American community with a black principal and
faculty.[49]

Cuney fought hard for establishing black colleges. He once sarcasti-
cally pointed out that "the only two public institutions open to him [and
other African Americans] are the penitentiary and the lunatic asylum."
In 1878 he supported the creation of Prairie View Agricultural and Mechanical College. Even after the creation of the school, Cuney remained
critical of using of public lands to support Texas A&M while the college
kept blacks from attending. His assistance in finding scholarships and
other financial help became his most important contribution to Prairie
View and later Paul Quinn, a private college founded by the Colored
Methodist Episcopal Church in 1881. Wade C. Rollins, treasurer of Prairie View shortly after Cuney's death, wrote to Maud: "Your father was
interested in this school and was instrumental in many ways in having a
large number of young colored men attend it, among them myself. He
secured for me a scholarship here for three successive years, and whatever
success I may have attained to this point, is in large measure due to his
kindness and foresight."[50]

In the early 1880s Prairie View became the principal provider of black
public-school teachers. Even with Prairie View, many black schools went

without adequate instructors. To promote more and better teachers, better schools, and higher salaries, Cuney and twelve other leading African Americans organized the Colored Teachers' State Association in 1884. Open to black educators and all other interested citizens, the association led the way for the improvement of black schooling. In an address to the new association, Cuney laid down the professional and moral tone he believed teachers should follow, stating: "The greatest work of training the minds of our youth, who are to aid in the work of solving the momentous problem of the status of the Negro on this continent, is a noble work. While it is, primarily, your duty to look after their mental training— yet you have still another and higher duty to perform—that of instilling into their minds a sensitive conscience."[51]

Wright Cuney was a man of unbounded energy and intellect. Almost nothing concerning black Texans seemed beyond his time or effort. He lobbied the legislature for the creation of the Deaf, Dumb, and Blind Institute for Colored Youth at Austin beginning in 1883 and continuing until its creation in 1887. Maud, after college graduation, taught at the institute for a short period. Whether in labor, civic, or educational activities, Cuney effectively represented the interests of black Texans. In Galveston he had the solid support of African Americans, which allowed him to pursue broader interests such as fighting corruption in city government that affected white as well as black citizens. By becoming an exponent of electricity and an improved water supply, he thought ahead of his time. During his four years as alderman, Cuney promoted the interests of the black community and gave black voters an important voice in city government before disfranchisement reduced their influence.

For black labor, he accomplished much by manipulating hostile racial attitudes. Once white employers allowed black screwmen into the skilled labor force on the harbor docks, they proved themselves as laborers. His leadership in protests of segregation did not stop the advance of Jim Crow, but it did give blacks a way to fight back and an outlet for their frustrations. Perhaps his greatest success came in improving black education in Galveston. Although white assumptions of black inferiority dominated their worldview, Cuney obtained impressive concessions that added to educational possibilities for African Americans in Galveston. He had an advantage over most of his white counterparts in that he had lived in the North before the Civil War and did not seem limited by the parochialism that characterized many in the city.

As an African American and as a political and civic leader, Wright
Cuney developed a multifaceted philosophy. While this developed in part
as a response to white prejudice, he could not avoid the influence of other
factors. He was the son of a white father who epitomized the paternalistic slaveholder. Cuney's civic and labor activities in some ways had a
paternalistic impulse, but they also went beyond a narrow elite view of
self-interest. As an educated black man with impressive political talents,
Cuney showed a commitment to provide leadership for African American
interests. He also had political ambitions that, if realized, would require
a strong base of support. Though most white businessmen in Galveston
voted Democratic, their work with Cuney on labor issues aided his civic
success. Thus, he created his base in Galveston not only among other
African Americans but also among white business leaders.

CHAPTER 3

Political Education, 1869–83

"IN TEXAS THE ACKNOWLEDGED LEADER of the party is a colored man, and the white republican—be he who he may—who attempts to relegate him to the rear will have undertaken a contract of no usual magnitude." James P. Newcomb, Republican leader of the "Lily White" movement in the 1880s, knew well the enormous political talents of his adversary, Norris Wright Cuney. Newcomb had watched with increasing consternation Cuney's rise through the ranks, backed by black support, during the 1870s. Following Reconstruction, African American politicians all across the South began to lose their precarious share of political power and influence, but Wright Cuney of Texas bucked the trend. His rise to power and his control of the Republican Party during the last two decades of the nineteenth century reflected his ability to learn quickly from older leaders, his successful service as their supporter, and his talent as an emerging leader in his own right.[1]

Only in his twenties during Reconstruction, Cuney until 1869 played a limited role in Republican politics. He used this time to hone his political skills. Cuney rose to leadership after Reconstruction, yet in many ways he was an extension of that process. Several influences aided him in his political education, but none appear more important than his mentor, George T. Ruby. In several ways Cuney continued the leadership role, ideas, and agenda set in motion by Ruby and black Texans during Reconstruction.

Cuney first met Ruby while working on the steamboat *Grey Eagle*, which made frequent stops at New Orleans during the Civil War. Later both men made their homes in Galveston, where Ruby established a political base among African Americans that Cuney eventually would inherit. Born in New York City in 1841 and well educated, Ruby had moved first to Louisiana and then to Texas, teaching in the Freedmen's Bureau schools. In 1867 the Reconstruction Acts called for constitutional conventions with delegations elected without regard to race, color, or previous condition. This gave blacks like Ruby and Cuney the opportunity to become politically active.[2]

Ruby proved to be an able debater and political organizer, demonstrating "responsibility and moderation" throughout his career. Along with James Newcomb and others, he helped establish the Texas Loyal Union League. The league, organized as a patriotic club in the North during the Civil War, expanded to the former Confederate states after the conflict. Organizers sought to educate African Americans in politics and to mobilize them as a political force. Ruby's influence within the league stretched well beyond Galveston. As registered voters, black males became the most important source of Republican electoral strength. Ruby, as the man who could deliver these votes, similarly grew in importance. He opened the door to party leadership through which Cuney later stepped.[3]

African Americans came to see political power as the best way to preserve their rights, but the "white power structure" allowed only limited access. Black registers signed up over forty-seven thousand African American voters before the constitutional convention. White Unionists needed black votes, but some did not want to share power. In 1867 Ruby decided to run for election as a delegate to the convention. Ruby's decision, and the decision of other blacks to participate actively as delegates and officeholders, created tension between whites and blacks within the party. These internal struggles characterized Texas Republicans for the remainder of the century. Of the ninety-two delegates elected to the convention, ten blacks, including Ruby, gained seats. Led by Ruby, and in the face of severe criticism by many whites and newspapers, blacks became very active in the convention, representing themselves well in the process. While this occurred, Cuney stayed in Galveston working on Ruby's behalf.[4]

Ideologically, most white Republicans represented prewar unionist sentiment. Some of them fought for the Confederacy, while many "continued to demonstrate, either actively or passively, their Union sympathies." Ending slavery and supporting human rights for African Americans seemed to be of less concern for most Texas unionists than it was for many of their northern counterparts. One in ten white Republican office-holders during Reconstruction held elective office before the war. These men considered it only natural that they assume leadership afterward. They did not necessarily consider that blacks also had a right to hold office. Unionists faced a complex problem. They knew they had to develop a program regarding the freedmen that would gain northern acceptance, but many refused to give up their own "prejudices and preconceptions about blacks." Most postwar white Republicans supported the idea of black participation as voters to maintain their own elective offices but did not favor blacks in leadership positions.[5]

After passage of the Reconstruction Acts and their subsequent registration, African Americans made up the majority in the Republican Party. The 1868 convention saw Ruby and other blacks support issues Cuney would continue to advocate later. Education represented an important issue for African Americans. They supported the development of a system of public education for both black and white children. Ruby pushed for the prevention of discrimination in public accommodations and other infringements of civil rights. Years later, as legal discrimination became a reality, Cuney fought to overturn such laws. Ruby supported investigations and proposed remedies for ending violence against blacks. Following Reconstruction, Cuney continued to support and expand upon this agenda.[6]

White Republicans at the convention split over *ab initio* (voiding the Texas Secession Ordinance) and a proposal to reestablish law and order by dividing Texas into two or three states. Factional disputes among whites developed into a major problem and remained so for much of the Reconstruction period. Gov. Elisha Pease, appointed to replace James W. Throckmorton, failed to provide the leadership necessary to unify the different views at the convention. African Americans did not have the luxury, however, of divisions among themselves. Although it ratified the Thirteenth and Fourteenth Amendments, the convention failed to act on a major concern for Ruby and other blacks, the disfranchisement of many ex-Confederates. The convention also failed to support a resolution proposed by Ruby and C. W. Bryant, another black delegate, condemning voter intimidation and bribery. Upset with the disfranchisement issue and the convention's failure to guarantee African American civil rights in Texas, Ruby resigned in protest.[7]

Organized violence directed against unionists and against African Americans increased demands within the league for punitive action.

Widespread violent acts against freedmen by their former masters characterized the years immediately following the war. Political activity by African Americans stirred white fears of black domination, especially after passage of the Reconstruction Acts and the formation of the Union League. In reaction, the Ku Klux Klan and other groups began a campaign of violence directed against politically active blacks. The U.S. Army and the Freedmen's Bureau tried to keep violence under control but suffered from severe manpower shortages. In 1868, for example, there were only twelve garrisons based around urban areas in Texas with just over thirteen hundred soldiers. During election periods, the protection efforts of the army and the bureau failed. Following Reconstruction, Cuney and black Republicans continued to face violence and threats of violence for their political activity. After an extensive study of inter-racial homicides in Texas following the Civil War, the constitutional convention appropriated twenty-five thousand dollars for the apprehension of criminals, but the Pease administration seemed reluctant to prosecute terrorists. Their failure to take forceful action against violent elements angered Ruby and other blacks within the Union League.[8]

Blacks realized they could not rely upon white actions to protect their interests but would have to take control of their own destinies. With few exceptions, even sympathetic whites failed to appreciate African American concerns. White leadership of the Union League seemed to take black membership for granted. Dissension among blacks within the league soon spread throughout the organization. The failure by the leadership to understand their concerns gave Ruby the opportunity in June, 1868, to secure from whites control of the state organization. Ruby's leadership of the league provided the electoral base from which Edmund J. Davis and the Radical Republicans came to power. Later Cuney expanded that base within the black community to achieve leadership of the Republican Party.[9]

At the Republican convention in Austin during August, 1868, Pease tried to maintain his tenuous hold on the party. With the support of the white delegate majority, Pease attempted to limit black participation. To counter this, Ruby, a consummate politician, formed an alliance with Edmund J. Davis, James P. Newcomb, and other white Republicans unhappy with Pease's leadership. By controlling the majority, Pease retained control of the convention but eventually lost leadership of the party. Davis and his supporters, sensing a possible victory at the polls was within their grasp, bolted the convention and formed a new Republican organization. This new group actively sought African American support by acceding to black demands for protection against terrorism and a public education system for both races.[10]

Pres. Ulysses Grant, unsure which side to support, delayed calling new elections until the fall of 1869. For the next year, both sides attempted to discredit the other. Compromise efforts met with little success. In a concerted effort to undermine Ruby's leadership, Pease supporters accused him of corruption and of selling out the Union League for personal gain. This only served to further alienate blacks. Although efforts to discredit Ruby failed, the league itself struggled to stay financially afloat. Local league organizations quickly ran out of money, and northern supporters failed to provide needed funds. Undeterred by personal attacks and organizational troubles, Ruby won a seat in the state senate for the Twelfth District, comprising Matagorda, Brazos, and Galveston Counties. Davis also won election as governor and Republicans obtained a majority in the legislature.[11]

Once in the state senate, Ruby suggested to Governor Davis the appointment of Cuney as sergeant-at-arms for the Twelfth Legislature. In his new position Cuney gained the friendship and respect of Governor Davis. Senator Ruby began to pursue a political strategy of attracting whites to the Republican Party. This too would have an effect on Cuney's career. Ruby had become the first to organize African American labor on the Galveston wharfs. The Negro Longshoremen's Benevolent Association organized unskilled dockworkers into Texas's first black union; the Screwmen's union later organized by Cuney grew out of this earlier organization. Ruby hoped for an alliance based on the interdependence between white business and black labor, tying the two groups to the Republican Party. Unfortunately, some suspicious whites viewed this as a blatant grab for power and an example of black domination.[12]

In the legislature Ruby sought to develop ties with Galveston's business community by supporting favorable bills on banking, insurance companies, and railroad interests. In pursuing such legislation Ruby cooperated with Democrats on railroad issues, though with few political benefits. Allocating scarce resources to business only lessened the resources available for black concerns. Many blacks within the Union League became displeased with Ruby's actions. They became further dissatisfied with the neglect shown by Republican congressman William T. Clark of the Third

District, which included Galveston. After being endorsed by Ruby, who then organized the votes necessary for his election, Clark promptly ignored black concerns. Ruby received the brunt of the black criticism for Clark's inaction. In a no-win situation, Ruby angered whites by supporting bills creating a public school system, a militia, and a state police force supported by blacks.[13]

Ruby probably expected white anger and distrust, but many blacks in the league failed to understand the necessity of Ruby's probusiness stance. Conservative Republicans who opposed Davis and Ruby helped fuel black dissatisfaction within the league. Louis Stevenson, a former white Freedmen's Bureau agent and league organizer, attempted to capitalize on black discontent and strip Ruby of his position within the organization. Stevenson also announced his intentions to run against Clark for Congress. In another surprise, he successfully captured the presidency of the Galveston Union League. Ruby fought back. James P. Newcomb, Ruby's successor as president of the state organization, allowed him a free hand in reorganizing the league, creating new charters, and revoking old ones. Ruby created a new Galveston chapter, supported the selection of Cuney as president, and revoked the charter of the old chapter. When Stevenson protested to the national office, Newcomb convinced headquarters to ignore his pleas. Realizing his difficulties with black voters, a contrite Congressman Clark conceded his mistakes and regained the support of Ruby and his followers.[14]

Because of his own political struggles and his efforts to retain power, Ruby began to share leadership with Cuney. In June, 1871, at the National Labor Convention of the Working Men of Texas held in Houston, Cuney became convention chairman. The National Labor Convention arose from a desire of the Republican Party to keep the National Labor Union from forming blacks into a labor party. Stevenson sought to gain labor support, but Cuney's tight control of the convention allowed Ruby time to work privately to unify labor union support behind Clark and Davis.[15]

Previously, Grant in 1869 had decided to support the Davis faction of Republicans, a decision that aided Ruby's career and as a result Cuney's career. The president appointed Nathan Patton, friend of both Ruby and Cuney, as collector of customs for the port of Galveston. Ruby became a special deputy collector. From this position, he controlled federal patronage for the Galveston area, rewarding party loyalists with appointments for the next four years. Cuney received three different posts. In

February, 1872, he obtained appointment as night inspector of customs. Unhappy in the position, perhaps because of the hours involved, Cuney resigned and became revenue inspector at Sabine Pass. He returned to the Galveston port as a daytime inspector in August, 1873.[16]

Ruby's control of patronage in Galveston aided Cuney in another way. Besides controlling federal patronage for Galveston, Ruby received from Governor Davis power over state patronage in that region as well. This included the prerogative of naming officials to the newly created public school system. At Ruby's request, Davis named party loyalist Capt. William H. Griffin as Galveston's supervisor of education. Griffin joined the Union League, headed by Cuney, and in July, 1871, named Nathan Patton, Ruby, and Cuney to the school board. Through these positions, Ruby and Cuney could reward other party loyalists with additional posts. Although these were political appointments, most observers believed Griffin highly qualified for the position. The *Galveston News* called Griffin "a genuine Radical" but also "a man of as good a moral character as can probably be found in the party." Cuney's continued interest in education included his participation at the founding of the Texas Colored Teacher's Association in 1884.[17]

The Stevenson faction, stymied in trying to take over the league and control the union, turned to the Third District Republican Convention in the summer of 1871. Stevenson supporters at county conventions obtained election as alternates hoping to contest Ruby's control at the district level. Ruby came well prepared for this meeting. Fearing Stevenson supporters might try to disrupt the convention, he requested that Davis send state police to maintain order. Ruby, who controlled the Credentials Committee, disqualified Stevenson supporters. Angry, Stevenson alternates tried to protest but without success as the state police forced them to their seats. Stevenson left the convention defeated, while many of his supporters rejoined Ruby's faction. Ruby and Cuney won unanimous election as delegates to the state Republican convention at Houston.[18]

Ruby won the factional disputes among blacks but failed to attract whites to the Republican fold. Realizing he could not win without white support, he decided against running for another senatorial term. In the 1871 election a large majority of blacks rallied around Ruby to vote for Clark, but Ruby's following among some African Americans appeared strained because of his strong-arm tactics at the convention. Clark failed to win reelection to Congress, which foreshadowed the defeat of Davis for governor in 1873, ending the Reconstruction process in Texas. To many, Ruby's political fortunes appeared tied to those of Governor Davis. Ruby considered his position in Texas untenable and moved to New Orleans shortly after the 1873 election, though he may have planned to leave Texas for some time. His previous actions clearly put his young protégé Wright Cuney in a position to become his successor as the leader of black Republicans.

Even before Ruby left Texas, Cuney began to act independently of his benefactor. At the Colored Men's Convention in July, 1873, Cuney, on his own merits, won the presidency of the organization. Under his leadership, the convention called for the passage of the civil rights bill being considered in Congress. The legislation, eventually passed in 1875, attempted to guarantee equal access to public accommodations, including hotels, transportation system, and schools. Blacks wanted not only civil rights protection but also to promote better relations with whites, who seemed especially concerned that blacks were demanding social equality. Cuney and the delegates sought to allay these fears. "We know perfectly well," the convention platform stated, "that a man's social relations cannot be made by legislative enactments." Cuney's dedication to civil rights did not waiver for the remainder of his career.[19]

The growing prominence of Cuney among black Republicans and in the African American community at large made him a target for political and personal attacks by Democrats. Cuney's immediate problem following the defeat of Davis came not from Democrats but from conservatives within his own party. After President Grant refused to intervene in 1874 to keep Governor Davis in office, Davis openly criticized Grant for causing a permanent break between the two men. In retaliation, Grant withdrew Davis's control over federal patronage, favoring more conservative Republicans instead. This action resulted in the replacement of Nathan Patton with Benjamin G. Shields in 1875 as the collector of customs at Galveston.[20]

Shields, an opinionated former Alabama state legislator with an anti-black bias, moved to Texas in the 1850s. From the beginning, Shields sought to replace Cuney as inspector of customs. When Cuney openly criticized him for his refusal to appoint blacks to patronage positions, Shields summarily dismissed him. Thus began the first of many battles Cuney had with conservative Republicans to maintain his federal employment and to protect his growing influence within the Republican Party.[21]

As news spread in Galveston of his dismissal, Cuney gained support from several unexpected sources; his civic activities had unanticipated results. By 1875, Cuney had begun to establish himself as a valuable citizen in the community. During the late 1860s and early 1870s, Galveston suffered from widespread corruption and criminal activity. The business community began a citywide reform movement hoping to rid their town of "unwanted" elements and to attract outside investments. Some of Galveston's leading businessmen and merchants formed a reform organization and asked Cuney to participate. According to R. L. Fulton, a future mayor, Cuney proved to be "an important influence in the reform movement that enabled us to rescue our city from hoodlumism that had so long held sway, and had wellnigh brought disgrace upon our fair city." The serving mayor, a Democrat, organized a petition drive, obtained over one hundred signatures from Galveston's "leading citizens," and requested the U.S. secretary of the treasury to reinstate Cuney. Additionally, the *Galveston Daily News,* a strongly Democratic paper, protested his dismissal, pointing out that "Cuney has shown himself to be above the average of his race—a friend of law and public tranquility." Following the intervention of city leaders, the Treasury Department ordered Cuney's reinstatement. Although Cuney's position now seemed secure, Shields continued to agitate for his removal.[22]

As Shields would soon learn, Cuney could also play political hardball. By 1876, Edmund J. Davis had lost the governorship and control over federal patronage, but he still controlled the party machinery. The black majority and Cuney remained loyal to the former governor until his death in 1883. Cuney's election to the state Platform Committee in 1872 and as secretary of the State Executive Committee in 1876 illustrated his growing importance to the party. Davis began to view Cuney as the de facto leader of black Republicans. The contentious state convention of 1876, like previous conventions, divided between conservatives and the Davis faction. Blacks, who made up 90 percent of party membership, made their presence felt. They supported a strong platform against the new state constitution and called for the enforcement of laws against the Ku Klux Klan. Conservatives in the minority had few successes. Cuney then turned the tables on his enemies by pushing through a resolution calling for the replacement of Shields and several other conservative federal officeholders.[23]

Infuriated with the resolution, Shields increased his efforts to remove Cuney. Shortly after the convention, Shields accused Cuney of malfea-

sance. Following an investigation, the Treasury Department absolved
Cuney of any wrongdoing. Shields became increasingly frustrated. He
personally wrote to the undersecretary of the treasury, telling of Cuney's
"duplicity and impudence" and asking for his removal "for reasons of
official decorum and common decency." Cuney responded with a letter
from Davis. The former governor accused Shields of recommending
Democrats for positions and unjustly attacking "one of our best colored
Republicans." Although his position was far from secure, Cuney continued to work as inspector, hoping the coming presidential election would
improve his position.[24]

In 1876 Cuney also made his first try for state office. At the Galveston
Senatorial District Convention, Cuney won by acclamation the nomination for state representative. He probably knew from the beginning
that his chances of winning would be slim, but the campaign allowed
him to establish his position on the issues with black voters. Cuney
opposed the new state Constitution of 1875 that replaced the Constitution
of 1869. The new document reversed much of what African Americans
had accomplished during Reconstruction. Education was a special
concern for him. Cuney opposed school segregation and favored
amending the constitution to levy "a specific tax for the support [of]
public education." He also favored lengthening the school term from six
to nine months and extending the "scholastic age from 7 to 18 years."
Disturbed with blacks being excluded from juries, Cuney also wanted
revision of jury laws "to the end that jurors may be drawn from the body
of the people." He also favored levying taxes to build juvenile institutions
"so [young offenders] will not be compelled to associate with hardened
criminals." Cuney's prolabor philosophy came through in his opposition
to the use of long-term convicts in building public roads. Instead, he
preferred the use of unemployed black labor. Although Cuney lost the
election, his forward-looking campaign helped solidify his black
following.[25]

At the state convention, Cuney won election as a delegate to the Republican National Convention held at Cincinnati, Ohio. The convention proved to be a watershed event in Cuney's political life. He began to
develop strong alliances and friendships with important Republican leaders, including Senators William B. Allison of Iowa, Samuel Fessenden of
Connecticut, Matthew Quay of Pennsylvania, and New York political
boss Thomas Platt. While in Cincinnati, Cuney met his political hero,

James G. Blaine. Cuney's long support for Blaine began after reading a speech he had given years earlier supporting black voting rights: "There is no protection you can extend to a man so effective and conclusive as the power to protect himself. And in assuring protection to the loyal citizens you assure permanency to the government. The bestowal of suffrage is therefore not merely the discharge of a personal obligation toward those who are enfranchised; but it is the most farsighted provision against social disorder, the surest guarantee of peace, prosperity and public justice."[26]

Cuney had read Blaine's speech at the impressionable age of twenty-one. The Civil War had concluded only two years earlier. Like blacks all across the South, Cuney struggled to establish a life after slavery. Unlike most African Americans at the time, he had the advantage of an education. Cuney knew of his white father's political background. As a youth working and playing in a household dominated by the noted politician, he probably overheard many political conversations. His two black mentors, P. B. S. Pinchback and George Ruby, had political ambitions. Blaine's speech and the federal grant of suffrage, no doubt, coalesced in Cuney's mind, making a political career seem possible. He believed that only through politics and the ballot could African Americans protect their newly established civil rights.[27]

The black Texan's support for the senator from Maine derived from what he thought Blaine represented. He did not have the advantage of hindsight for a clear assessment of Blaine's character. Judging by the senator's later statements and actions, his actual support for African Americans appears suspect and, at times, opportunistic. His speech at the time may have represented a desire by Blaine to capitalize upon sectional tensions to advance his own career. He did not, for example, favor appointing African Americans to diplomatic posts. When Blaine as secretary of state appointed blacks at all, it was only on a token basis. The one appointment he could not escape was Frederick Douglass as ambassador to Haiti in 1889, one that he made reluctantly. When Douglass resigned because of Blaine's antagonism, Blaine opposed naming another African American to the position. Pres. Benjamin Harrison, under intense political pressure from blacks, proposed to replace Douglass with John S. Durham, a black journalist. In a letter to the president, Blaine reluctantly relented: "I had hoped that a white man might be taken but as you seem to think you are bound to appoint a colored man, this will be the easiest way out of it and will put a Minister in Port au Prince much sooner than any other way. Its best effect will be that it will stop the colored applicants by giving them a man of their own color, greatly superior to any other one of them." What Blaine thought of Cuney is difficult to determine, but Cuney's support for Blaine never wavered. No doubt, Cuney hoped Blaine would reward him for his years of support, but the relationship appears to have been one sided. In 1889, for example, Harrison was considering Cuney for the job of collector of customs for the port of Galveston. Blaine, at least publicly, neither supported nor opposed Cuney's application.[28]

Cuney's closest political alliance and friendship to develop out the 1876 convention came with James S. "Ret" Clarkson, an influential editorial writer for the *Des Moines Register.* Raised in a devout Methodist and abolitionist family that operated a station in the underground railroad before the Civil War, Clarkson strongly supported the idea of black equality. He proudly considered himself a Radical Republican. Like Cuney, he became a strong supporter of James G. Blaine. Clarkson held a number of federal and party positions, including vice chairman of the Republican National Committee and first assistant postmaster general. Both positions provided him considerable influence over federal patronage. Later this alliance proved very valuable for Cuney's career.[29]

Before the convention, many Republicans believed Blaine to be the front-runner for their presidential nomination, but as at other times in his career, Blaine's name became linked to scandal. Reports suggested he had sold some worthless stock of a defunct Arkansas railroad to the Union Pacific for sixty-four thousand dollars. As the convention began, Blaine was appearing before a congressional committee investigating the matter. A similar controversy had involved possible complicity by Blaine in the 1872 Credit Mobilier affair, but as with the 1876 charges, a congressional investigation found no incriminating evidence. After the well-publicized scandals of the Grant administration, delegates preferred a candidate with "clean hands" and chose Rutherford B. Hayes.[30]

The election of Hayes in the controversial election of 1877 would cost Cuney his position in the collector's office. Northern sentiment had tired of the so-called "Negro problem" and no longer supported the protection of southern black rights. As president, Hayes began to alter Republican policy in the South. In effect, he abandoned African Americans, who composed most of the southern membership of the Republican Party.

Hayes pursued a two-prong strategy of conciliating white southerners while attempting to attract dissident and moderate Democrats into the Republican fold. Federal patronage became a major tool in this approach. In most southern states the administration excluded blacks from consideration for federal employment. Often the administration replaced existing black federal officeholders with conservative white Republicans or Democrats. Speaking to an Atlanta meeting of black Republicans, President Hayes told the stupefied audience that "their rights and interest would be safer if the great mass of intelligent white men were let alone by the general government."[31]

Shields took advantage of this new federal posture to eliminate his adversary. John Sherman, the new treasury secretary, received a number of letters from Shields asking for the removal of Cuney. Again, Governor Davis tried to intervene on Cuney's behalf. Davis wrote James Newcomb, then in Washington pursuing his own hopes for a federal position, and asked that he see Sherman to convince him to keep Cuney. Newcomb, already viewing Cuney as a rival, apparently did not act on Davis's request. Nonetheless, the Hayes administration was eager to institute its new policy. Sherman obliged Shields's request and on July 25, 1877, officially approved the removal of Cuney. Afterward, the Treasury Department issued its rationale for his dismissal. In a virulent report, with few facts, a treasury official characterized Cuney as "a man of no culture, has no qualifications as a clerk nor for general business, and is a genuine professional politician."[32]

Cuney's fight with Shields won the admiration of both friends and opponents. Most knew he would rebound from the setback. The new governor, Democrat Richard Coke, had no doubts, noting that "Cuney is a spry sort of a fellow." But following Reconstruction, Cuney and black Texans increasingly faced a hostile political environment. While the African American population in Texas continued to expand, the white population grew even faster, aided by increased migration from other southern states. By 1880, black Texans made up 90 percent of the Republican Party but only 25 percent of the population. According to historian Alwyn Barr, black politicians now had three choices: "They could seek greater control over policy and patronage within the Republican party; they could join or attempt 'fusion' with dissident Democratic factions or third parties; or they could, by the 1890s, support the Democratic party in an effort to influence its policies."[33]

That analysis aptly describes Cuney's future political course. He above all considered himself a loyal Republican and often sublimated his personal ambitions to that of the party. The good of party, as he saw it, dominated most of his political actions. Similarly, Cuney believed what was good for the party would be good for "his people." Like many African Americans in the late twentieth century, who now identify their future with that of the Democratic Party, Cuney in the late nineteenth century identified black aspirations with the Republican Party. He supported any effort, including fusion, to advance the party. While Cuney considered Democrats anathematic to black interests, he did not preclude cooperating with dissident elements within that party in hopes of influencing or changing prevalent Democratic policies.

Late-nineteenth-century America, especially the South dominated by one political party, became a hotbed of independent and third-party activity. During a national depression in the late 1870s, farm prices fell dramatically. As a result many farmers, especially members of the Grange movement, grew dissatisfied with both political parties. Disgruntled elements in Texas and throughout the South began to organize the Greenback Party. Greenback inflationary ideas of increasing the money supply to help pay off mounting agricultural debts appealed to both white and black farmers. The new party called for an end to convict labor and supported a public school system that had a direct appeal to black voters. Black independents and many black Republicans, especially farmers, supported the Greenback cause. Organizational strength in Texas derived from individual clubs formed across the state. Seventy of the 482 clubs organized in 1878 represented black membership.[34]

Known for his "unimpeachable republicanism," Cuney believed strongly in basic nineteenth-century Republican ideology of high tariffs and "sound money" policy. Nothing would have pleased him more than a Republican victory at the polls, but he knew that would not be possible in Texas. While opposing Greenback "easy money" policy, he could support the party's labor and education issues. As his unfolding career had illustrated, Cuney would employ any means necessary to maintain the viability of the Republican Party while hopefully weakening that of the Democrats. Cuney began to excel at political manipulation. Besides, he may have reasoned, why alienate black Republicans already in the Greenback camp. Former governor Davis, who headed the state executive committee, also knew Republicans had little chance of winning statewide office in 1878. Cuney urged Davis to support a fusion effort. At their insistence, the executive committee voted not to put forward a ticket and to support the Greenback Party.[35]

Dissident Republicans led by conservative A. B. Norton, a bitter enemy of Davis, called for a special "consultation" held in lieu of a convention. Representatives from approximately forty counties met at Austin in October and, not surprisingly, nominated Norton for governor. In an attempt to keep blacks in the Republican fold, the ad hoc convention nominated Richard Allen for lieutenant governor. Among black leaders within the Republican Party, only Allen could possibly challenge Cuney for dominance with other African Americans.[36]

Allen had come to Texas as a slave in 1837. After emancipation, he became an agent for the Freedmen's Bureau, helped organize the Republican Party in Harris County, and served as a vice president of the Union League. With little formal education, Allen became a successful contractor, a member of the Twelfth Legislature, and collector for the port of Houston. In the late 1870s he became a spokesman for the ill-fated black "exodus" movement. Although Allen appeared well known by black Republicans, he lacked a broad base of support. He tended to be opportunistic in his political approach, often telling "each audience what it wished to hear, thereby throwing constraints of consistency and intellectual honesty to the wind." In the 1878 election Norton and Allen came in a distant third behind the Democrats and Greenbacks.[37]

Many blacks found that their loyalty to the Republican Party outweighed the attraction of the Greenbacks. These African Americans believed they could best protect their interests within the party. This loyalty did not exclude support for the fusion efforts of Cuney and Davis, though. Black Republicans who voted for the Greenback Party considered themselves loyalists. Politically active African Americans, who just thirteen years earlier could not take part in the political process, had through necessity become as sophisticated as their white counterparts. The first fusion effort went down to defeat, but many blacks realized a possible path to victory. Democrats, however, while never recognizing "Negro" sophistication in any form, feared this might be the case as well. In a time when political polling did not exist and Democrats had no way of determining the strength of the opposition, fear often drove their response. Fear also led to increased antagonism toward blacks and their leadership.

Besides white-led intimidation, sporadic violence, and discrimination, black economic opportunity grew at a very slow rate. When in 1879 rumors spread throughout the South that free land was available for the taking in Kansas, many African Americans jumped at the opportunity. In Mississippi over six thousand blacks gathered at river docks trying to catch a boat to Missouri and then to Kansas. Black Texans reacted more cautiously, until May. At a national convention of African Americans held in Nashville and attended by Richard Allen and Wright Cuney, Allen spoke forcefully in favor of the exodus. This gave many blacks hope that the rumors were true, and as many as twelve thousand black Texans may have migrated to Kansas by December. Many soon became discouraged when the rumors proved false, and they began to return to Texas.[38]

There would be additional emigration movements and plans developed throughout the remainder of the century. One involved William H. Ellis, a close friend and supporter of Wright Cuney. The prosperous black San Antonio "hides and wool" merchant received a large land grant from the Mexican government. He promised to colonize ten thousand blacks in the Tlahualilo area near Durango. Ellis, perhaps too optimistic, planned for the emigrants to turn the desert area into small fertile cotton plantations. He hired R. A. "Pegleg" Williams, a less-than-reputable Atlanta emigration agent, to colonize over five thousand African Americans by 1895. During 1894 and 1895, more than two thousand black southerners made the trip to Mexico. Amid reports of death and starvation, the effort quickly dissolved, with surviving emigrants returning to the States. Most other emigration efforts also failed.[39]

Nineteenth-century emigration efforts received a mixed reaction from black leaders. In the *New Orleans Observer*, George Ruby wrote strongly worded articles against violence perpetrated by whites against blacks and urged emigration as a way to escape "lawless acts." Others, like P. B. S. Pinchback, denounced political and economic conditions but fell short of endorsing the movement, calling for economic reforms instead.

Cuney, unlike other black leaders, still held a position of political prominence. While he sympathized with black emigrants, an exodus from Texas would only weaken the Republican Party. He wrote long letters discouraging emigration and publicly criticized those who did otherwise. He considered himself a patriotic American first and a "son of Texas" second. Cuney cautioned blacks to have patience. "Because an oligarchy now governs the South," Cuney wrote, "doesn't mean it always will, it is contrary to the genius of our constitution and laws." He incorporated in his philosophy a strong belief in black self-help, hope, and optimism. For those African Americans who had "become impatient at the injustice done them on the part of the American people and feel they can better their condition by going elsewhere," Cuney suggested they stay where they were and make the necessary sacrifices to obtain prosperity. "It is true, the clouds are lower over our Southland . . . yet I do know that we are not without hope." To those African Americans wanting to leave the United States permanently, Cuney counseled each to "carve out his own character, which will demand proper recognition here as soon as elsewhere." While Cuney would have disagreed with Booker T. Washington's stance on black political involvement, much of what he said about self-help echoed Washington's ideals.[40]

During 1880 the possibility of a large-scale black exodus from Texas subsided. Support for the Greenback Party seemed to be receding as Republicans prepared for the coming national convention. Davis and many of his followers remained bitter about the cooperation of the Hayes administration with southern Democrats. According to Davis, "no Republican here is respectable unless he is nincumpoop [sic] enough to curry favor with the Democracy and get their endorsement." Cuney appeared more sanguine about the party, especially after the new collector of customs at Galveston, his old adversary E. M. Pease, recommended him for an inspector position. He also hoped Blaine would receive the party's presidential nomination. Within the Texas delegation, other candidates gained more support. John Sherman of Ohio sought Texas delegates, but former president Grant gained the support of the majority. At the national convention, most black delegates, other than Cuney, supported the former Reconstruction president; Grant may have been a less than stellar president, but he had supported black civil rights. Cuney, however, had his mind set on the future. The majority of Texas delegates cast thirty-five ballots for Grant, while Cuney cast his for Blaine. On the thirty-sixth ballot, a shift of Blaine and Sherman delegates, including Cuney, helped nominate James A. Garfield. Cuney apparently did not pressure other delegates to vote for Blaine.[41]

Statewide elections in 1880 saw the Republicans regain their status as the second major party. Davis, the gubernatorial nominee, received a respectable 64,000 votes, a tally that nevertheless showed Republican weakness when compared to the 160,000 votes for Democrat O. M. Roberts. The Greenbacks came in third but reelected George Washington Jones to Congress. A complicated scenario developed in 1882. After Garfield's assassination, his successor, Chester A. Arthur, openly supported fusion efforts in the South as a way to build up Republican strength. Cuney could not have agreed more. He decided to exercise a leadership role in this fusionist effort. Davis, who found Arthur a more agreeable president than Hayes, strongly supported fusion. He also decided to run for Congress. The president urged Texas Republicans to support Jones as their candidate for governor.[42]

G. W. "Wash" Jones had moved to Texas at the age of twenty in 1848. Although a unionist and supporter of Stephen A. Douglas, with the coming of war Jones enlisted in the Confederate Army as a private and rose to the rank of colonel. Following the war, he became politically active. Jones served for a short time as lieutenant governor before Gen. Philip Sheridan removed him as an "impediment to Reconstruction." As a fusion candidate, he won election to Congress in 1878 and reelection in 1880. Jones may have been a former Confederate officer, but his political opinions seemed attractive to many Republicans. He supported "free schools, free ballot boxes, free opinion, free speech, and a free press; enforcement of the federal laws in the South"; and believed Texas should imitate northern economic policies. Jones openly courted black voters with his support for allowing blacks to serve on juries and for extending the school term.[43]

The overwhelming majority of black delegates to the 1882 state convention followed Cuney's leadership. Most of the white delegates remained loyal to Davis. Cuney's election as convention chairman illustrated his growing strength within the party. "In the interest of what we conceive to be liberal and progressive government," a convention resolution stated its support for "candidates who come before the people for suffrage as Independents." After deciding against placing a ticket in the field, the convention established a committee headed by Cuney to decide who to support. Not surprisingly, Jones received the nod. Cuney also decided to make another try for the state legislature. Besides campaigning for himself, he participated in the Jones campaign. He traversed the state, speaking to Republicans and African Americans on behalf of Jones. Although Jones lost, the fusion effort produced the highest anti-Democratic vote totals since the Civil War, with fusionists receiving over 40 percent of the vote.

In a legislative district where Democrats outnumbered Republicans three to one, Cuney came in a distant second for the legislature.[44]

Less than a year after the 1882 election, the old Republican warhorse Edmund J. Davis died, setting the stage for a new era in Texas Republicanism. As governor, Davis earned the respect and loyalty of black Republicans. He also became the focal point of everything Texas Democrats found repugnant in the Reconstruction process. As party leader he felt abandoned by the national organization and saw the party weakened by a resurgent "Democracy." He also faced conservative Republicans, who believed party leadership should naturally reside in the hands of whites, determined to take back leadership from him and his black allies. Davis's personality and leadership style often put him at odds with national party leaders who otherwise would have been allies. His successor had the personality and experience to be an able politician, but he was a man burdened with many of the same enemies and by the color of his skin.

The emerging leadership of Wright Cuney in the Texas Republican Party illustrates the path other African American politicians might have followed had Reconstruction succeeded. For the next fourteen years, he would lead that organization. George Ruby set the stage for Cuney's emergence. Ruby established him in numerous leadership positions and introduced him to Texas party leaders, most importantly Edmund J. Davis. After Ruby left Texas, Cuney inherited his political base but without all of his political baggage; Ruby had become unalterably linked to Davis. Cuney, as Ruby's younger protégé, received less notice and identification with Reconstruction, but he identified himself with most of Ruby's policies and goals that represented an overall black agenda.

Cuney also learned valuable lessons from Ruby's successes and failures. He succeeded in forming lasting alliances with the Galveston business community, resulting in the employment of hundreds of African Americans. Where Ruby failed to form powerful alliances with national party leaders, Cuney succeeded. He had a natural affinity and love of Texas and its history that Ruby lacked. Cuney's loyalty to Davis kept him from exerting greater leadership of black Republicans while the former governor lived. His political instincts may have led him to compromise with his opponents where Davis and Ruby had refused. As a Texan and former slave, Cuney could identify more closely with his fellow black Texans than could either Davis as a white man or Ruby as a free northern black. Unlike Ruby, who made Galveston primarily his political base, Cuney became an important member of the larger community. The respect shown Cuney by prominent men in the community and the alliances he formed with national figures in his party helped him become an influential political leader.

CHAPTER 4

New Leader of the Party

IN HIS SEMINAL STUDY, *Politics: Who Gets What, When, How,* political scientist Harold D. Lasswell states: "the study of politics is the study of influence and the influential. The influential are those who get the most of what there is to get. Those who get the most are elite; the rest are mass." Entering 1884, the Texas Republican Party seemed almost irrelevant to the political process. The possibility of a Republican winning statewide office appeared virtually impossible. African Americans formed 90 percent of the party membership but made up only 25 percent of the state population. Edmund Davis, the primary Republican leader since Reconstruction, had died. Internal dissension threatened to erode an already weak institution. Out of the chaos, Wright Cuney rose to leadership. He faced the challenge of making the Republican Party a viable institution. In so doing Cuney became an influential politician who the got the most there was to get for his party and for himself.[1]

Cuney used his considerable political skills to maneuver Republicans into the best possible position. He pursued fusion when he deemed it necessary and compromise with conservative Republicans when no viable fusion effort seemed possible. Since Republican prospects of winning Texas for the national ticket appeared remote, Cuney strove to make his state's delegations to national conventions influential in picking presidential nominees. In 1889 Cuney became collector of customs for the port of Galveston, the most important appointment any black would receive in the South. From this position he exerted enormous influence over Texas' political patronage. His party did not win statewide office during his tenure, but he made it and himself influential in the Texas political process.

Over fourteen years, from 1884 to 1897, Cuney faced enormous obstacles. Racially prejudiced white Republicans, who chaffed at the idea of black leadership, conspired to discredit and replace the majority's representative. Democrats contrived to eliminate African Americans from the election process altogether. Newspapers and white political leaders assailed Cuney in an almost constant barrage of erroneous and racist propaganda. In his private life, his wife, Adelina, grew increasingly ill with tuberculosis. Through it all, Cuney remained an optimist. He held on to party leadership and relished the political combat. He raised his children in a comfortable and loving environment, sending both to northern colleges and aiding other blacks in doing the same. Cuney maintained his position within the community and earned the respect of his fellow Galvestonians. Finally, in 1897, Cuney lost his leadership position. He also suffered from the illness that killed his wife the year before, but until his death on March 3, 1897, he remained optimistic that he could regain party leadership.

Cuney's leadership position existed through the will of the black majority. Beginning in the 1880s, most southern states began to experiment with the poll tax, grandfather clauses, educational qualifications, and a variety of other restrictive laws written to disfranchise black voters. According to historian J. Morgan Kousser: "each state became in effect a laboratory for testing one device or another. Indeed, the cross-fertilization and coordination between the movements to restrict the suffrage in the Southern states amounted to a public conspiracy." The Texas legislature tended to be slower in enacting such laws, although some lawmakers tried. Four years earlier, A. W. Terrell introduced a poll-tax bill in the Texas Senate to keep poor blacks from voting. The measure failed to pass. Not until 1902 did the legislature pass a poll tax that, along with the establishment of white primaries, eliminated most African Americans from the polls. Until that time blacks maintained their majority in the Republican Party.[2]

For African Americans, Cuney became the one bright spot in an increasingly dim political future. Blacks viewed his prominence with pride. Democrats and some white Republicans criticized blacks for "blindly following Wright Cooney," but such racially biased attacks held little sway within the black community. "We follow him," explained one African

American, "not because he is the Negro's 'Boss,' as termed by his enemies, nor because we fear him, but because we love him and wish to do him honor; and because he has done, is doing, can do, and will do more to bring the Negro of Texas into prominence than any man in the state." Even some Democrats praised Cuney for his "honesty." Others, like Democratic state senator James Clairborn, commented that although of "Negro blood," Cuney was "respected by the majority of the better thinking classes of the Anglo-Saxons."[3]

Charismatic and easy going, Cuney appeared as a "slender figure, five feet ten, straight black hair and mustache, black eyes; high cheek bones." He made friends easily. Even many of Cuney's strongest critics found it difficult to dislike him as a person. Cuney was, according to one Democratic newspaper, "A representative man, well informed, courteous, collected and with marked opinions on state and national politics. . . . It may be possible that he has not modesty, but he well succeeds in assuming that virtue if he has not." The *New York Sunday Press* described him as a "gentleman with a pleasant, clean cut face and a pair of eyes that look into one's soul; a well made man, full of vigor and the champion of his race in the far southwest; brawny, active, well read on current topics and an honor to the Republicans of Texas." The *New York Tribune* reported the respect shown the "colored man" by influential whites. The paper noted that, on one of Cuney's visits to the Hoffman House in New York, "one of the largest merchants in the South, Leon Blum, walking in the corridor, discovered Cuney, of whose presence in New York he was unaware and coming over to greet him with a handshake and cordiality that denoted both respect and esteem."[4]

Ideas of white supremacy required a rationale for any form of African American success. Therefore, part of Cuney's stance among whites who held him in higher regard than other African Americans derived in part from his lighter skin color. Newspapers and many individuals used this feature to account for Cuney's success, variously describing him as a "bright olive complexioned gentleman," of having an appearance "more like that of a Spaniard than a black man," or that "his features, hair and lanky figure seem to show a mixture of Indian and Spanish blood." According to the *St. Louis Republican:* "One of the ablest and most influential men of African blood in the South, . . . Cuney looks more like a Mexican than a Negro. He is tall and slim, and his hair is black and straight. He is about two-thirds Caucasian and one-third African." Many observers suggested his political success resulted entirely because of his Anglo blood. One newspaper bluntly stated, "Cuney is three-fourths white and one-fourth Nigger and the white part accounts for the brains in his head."[5]

Despite white views about his intelligence and skin color, Cuney viewed himself as a black man. As party leader, Cuney struggled mightily to maintain black Republicans as an important part of the political process. His first move to obtain leadership in his own right began at the Galveston County Convention on April 3, 1884. There he took on and won his first battle against A. G. Malloy. Earlier, Malloy had removed Cuney as inspector of customs; since then the dislike between the two men had become palpable. Because he held the most important federal position in Texas, Malloy in effect became the leader of those white Republicans opposed to Cuney. He and other white officeholders wanted to protect their positions and wanted desperately to see Chester Arthur returned to the White House. Distrustful and unimpressed by President Arthur's lukewarm support for southern blacks, Cuney hoped to see his hero James G. Blaine obtain the presidency. Cuney dominated the county convention, refusing to allow Malloy and his supporters to become delegates to the state meeting. He wanted very much to send as many delegates as he could to the national convention for Blaine.[6]

In a harbinger of battles to come, Republicans arrived at the state convention in Fort Worth in the midst of severe thunderstorms. Malloy and his supporters came prepared to challenge the seating of black delegates. According to one white delegate, "the color line will not be countenanced." Blacks such as Richard Allen expressed no desire to draw a color line but were "firm in demanding substantial recognition of their numerical strength in the state." John DeBruel, Cuney's fellow Mason and an ally, put it more succinctly, "We don't intend for a few officeholders to run the party in Texas any longer." Before the convention, many observers and newspapers expressed confidence that the "white officeholders" would control the convention. Cuney's name seemed to carry little importance in the preconvention reporting. Most whites simply refused to believe a black man could gain leadership. According to one newspaper, "The day has not arrived when a Negro can be the leader of even the Republican party in Texas."[7]

Events on the first day of the convention appeared to bear out that opinion. Whites still controlled the party apparatus. Besides dominating the Credentials Committee, they successfully elected J. C. DeGress as temporary chairman of the convention. DeGress had the respect of many blacks, but in an ironic twist, some black Republicans born and reared in Texas considered him a carpetbagger. More out of frustration than any real objection to northern immigrants, these blacks believed DeGress was forced upon them by the white minority. According to one angry delegate, "Shackles have been thrown around free citizens and the convention placed under the rule of carpet-baggers." Objecting to the "tones of contempt to carpetbaggers," DeGress responded that "as for myself I am here as a soldier." Newspapers took his chairmanship to mean a total victory of whites over black Republicans. The *Galveston Daily News* declared, "Spoils are triumphant, and captured the whole thing, gate, money, stakes and prizes."[8]

Over the years, Cuney found DeGress annoying and unreliable. Born in Prussia in 1842, Jacob DeGress immigrated to the United States in 1852. During the war he served under General Grant, obtaining the rank of lieutenant colonel; wounds received at Vicksburg would eventually cause his death in 1894. DeGress came to Texas following the war as an assistant commissioner of the Freedman's Bureau. Politically ambitious, he resigned from the bureau in 1870 when Governor Davis appointed him state superintendent of education. A strong believer in black education, DeGress served African Americans in Texas well. He became mayor of Austin before President Garfield appointed him postmaster. Always the opportunist, he would support either Cuney or his opponents whenever he considered it advantageous to do so. In 1884 DeGress believed his bread to be buttered on the anti-Cuney side of the loaf.[9]

On the second and third days of the convention, Cuney and the black majority proved the political pundits wrong. Delegates repeatedly called for Cuney to speak during the proceedings, leaving little doubt who they wanted as leader. They also clearly supported Blaine for president. Cuney chose when to speak carefully, with the most important moment following the report of the Credentials Committee. Whites controlled the majority on the committee, limited debate, and voted over vociferous objections to seat the Malloy delegation over Cuney's. When the committee announced its decision, blacks erupted in a pandemonium of protest. Webster Flanagan, an Arthur supporter but one who favored Cuney's leadership, "moved that a minority report be substituted" seating Cuney's regular delegation. DeGress tried and failed to rule him out of order. After a prolonged demonstration by black delegates for Cuney, he rose to speak. He denigrated those in the convention who had appealed to "race prejudice." Cuney urged the delegates not to turn over leadership of the convention to Malloy and other white officeholders. "Let not color be a bar to positions of honor and trust, but let merit alone be the test by which they are filled." Knowing that many if not most black delegates supported Blaine for the Republican nomination, Cuney warned the convention that he knew "on good authority" the Malloy contingent intended to vote for Arthur.[10]

Fearing a personal rebuke by the delegates, Malloy chose someone else to speak in his place. Unmoved by the opposing argument, the Cuney faction easily carried the day, 247 to 203. In a conciliatory move on the third and final day, Cuney allowed whites without opposition to name J. G. Tracy as permanent convention chairman. With blacks in total control, the final day lacked the controversy of the preceding two. The most important task remaining was the election of four delegates-at-large to the national convention. Those chosen would illustrate the strength of the black majority and which presidential candidate most state delegates supported. The convention named two blacks, Cuney and Richard Allen, and two whites, C. C. Binckley and Robert Zapp. Cuney and Zapp favored Blaine, Binckley leaned toward Blaine, and Allen favored Arthur. The *Galveston Daily News* reported "two-thirds" of the state delegates supported Blaine for president, but the convention itself did not instruct the delegation to vote for any particular candidate. Afterward, many whites began to form white Republican clubs to counter "black domination."[11]

Although the convention rejected Malloy's leadership, the *Galveston Daily News* praised him as "one of the best and most skillful of political fighters." Cuney, though, "is a queer problem without a particle of personal magnetism about him—unconsciously repellant in many of his traits of character and modes of action." Malloy would continue his challenge at the national convention. There the power of the incumbent president allowed the seating of Malloy and another pro-Arthur delegate from Texas. Even with this surprising development, Cuney promised that fourteen of Texas' twenty-eight delegates would vote for Blaine. Cuney also received his first position in the Republican hierarchy: vice president of the Committee on Permanent Organization. In 1886 Cuney became national committeeman and served in that position through 1896.[12]

Many delegates, including several from Texas, reported attempts by the Arthur camp to bribe them, reporting offers of between $350 and

$1,000 for votes. Being the incumbent could not save Arthur, however, in one of the few times in U.S. history when a political party denied a sitting president the opportunity for reelection. The "Plumed Knight" received the Republican nomination on the fourth ballot, with fifteen votes from the Texas delegation. Cuney became one of a select committee chosen by the convention to notify Blaine of his nomination at his Augusta, Maine, estate. Following the convention, one newspaper described Malloy as "a dead cock in the pit."[13]

At the convention Cuney not only proved himself as an admirable political adversary but also as a man willing to stand up for himself in other ways. In the lobby of his hotel, an old adversary and "a half dozen Chicago hoodlums" confronted Cuney. A former customs official from Texas named Bissell attempted to assault him. According to the *Galveston Daily News:* "Mr. Cuney advised him to go away, turning contemptuously away from him. As he did so, Bissell attempted to strike him with his cane, when Cuney caught him quickly by the arm and thrashed him unmercifully. Bissell finally called for mercy and sneaked out of the hotel." A Democratic newspaper praised Cuney for "pluck as well as brains." After his meeting with Blaine, Cuney returned home to a hero's welcome. A large band accompanied hundreds of torch-bearing African Americans who paraded down Galveston's Avenue L. "We were splendidly entertained in Maine; and our visit to Mr. Blaine was made very agreeable," Cuney told the audience.[14]

Cuney returned confident Blaine would beat Grover Cleveland, the Democratic candidate. Reporters and other observers now realized that if Blaine won, Cuney would become the most powerful Republican in the state. They wanted to know how a Blaine presidency would affect political patronage in Texas: "Why, of course, there will be some changes, but not a clean sweep as the public seems to think. Yes, I rather think there will be a change in the Galveston collectorship. What do I expect for myself? Oh, nothing, nothing. I am only a private citizen and have sought only do to my share in public matters toward my race and party. I would indeed feel it a compliment if the collectorship were offered me; it is the highest office the government can give in the state outside the judiciary; but I am trying to build up my private business and expect to stick to that." His response reflected his determination to eliminate Malloy while trying to allay other white officeholders' fear of a wholesale replacement, but he did make known his desire for the collectorship. His statement also reflected a basic trait that characterized his political career: a dedication to both race and party. But for 1884 at least, the question of Cuney patronage became mute when Blaine lost to Cleveland.[15]

In September the state convention met to decide whether to place a "straight-out" or a fusion ticket in the governor's race. As the recognized leader of the party by the black majority and the national organization, Cuney favored fusion with independents again led by Wash Jones. A realist, Cuney believed fusion provided the only chance for victory. He also hoped to attract independents to the Republican Party and to the Blaine candidacy. Republicans voted overwhelmingly, 308 to 80, to support backing Jones. White opponents bolted the convention. They knew the chance of winning without fusion appeared impossible but refused to accept black leadership. Bolters held their own convention, excluded all African Americans, and nominated A. B. Norton for governor. In the election Norton came in a distant third, while Jones and Blaine made a strong if unsuccessful showing at the polls.[16]

Cuney and Galveston Republicans faced another problem in that pivotal year. Thomas P. Ochiltree, Republican member of Congress from the Seventh District, which included Galveston, decided not to run for reelection. Ochiltree came from a well-known Texas political family; his father, William B. Ochiltree, was a respected Whig politician and a founder of the Texas Republic who had served in various elected and judicial positions. During the Civil War, Tom Ochiltree served on the staff of four different generals, including James Longstreet. Following the war, he joined the Republican Party and developed close ties with U. S. Grant and Speaker Thomas Reed. He also became one the best "stump speakers" in Texas and won election to Congress in 1882. Many white Republicans wanted Ochiltree to challenge Cuney for leadership within the party, but he sided with Cuney. Ochiltree called the white officeholders "an organized gang of blackmailers, consummate scoundrels, who are a disgrace to the party."[17]

Ochiltree had become an important booster for Galveston's economic growth in Congress. Civic leaders, including some Democrats, wanted him to remain in office for that reason alone. Leaders especially wanted a strong presence in Congress to obtain a federal appropriation for the construction of a deep-water harbor. Following the war, Galveston quickly became one of the largest ports in the South, eventually surpassing all other U.S. ports in cotton shipments. The development of new and larger ships made a deep harbor essential to continued growth. Many, including Alderman Cuney and others on the city council, believed Ochiltree provided the best chance for passage of a deep-harbor appropriation by Congress. Cuney promised to deliver black votes and campaign vigorously on his behalf, but Ochiltree refused to reconsider. The former congressman moved to New York City and continued to influence Texas affairs from a distance. Republicans chose a longtime Cuney friend and ally, Judge J. B. Rector, to run against Democrat William Crain. Both parties supported the idea of a deep harbor.[18]

At the 1886 state convention, Cuney sought to achieve a more harmonious party gathering. He pushed through the noncontroversial A. J. Rosenthal as permanent chairman. The new chairman, Cuney believed, would neither draw the ire of whites nor provide a target for Democratic attacks. Besides, Cuney reasoned, "the Republican convention had no marshallships or postoffices to dish out, hence the selection of a chairman of a state convention signified nothing." For this reason more than anything else, whites who bolted in 1884 remained within the regular organization.[19]

Fusion, another divisive factor, would not be an issue. With the end of the depression in 1879 and specie resumption, the Greenback Party no longer had unifying concerns and now appeared to be dying. Most Greenbacks returned to the Democratic Party. Cuney allowed A. M. Cochran, a leader of the white rebellion in 1884, to obtain the Republican nomination for governor. As the Republicans went down to ignominious defeat in 1886, Cuney could at least take comfort in knowing that a political opponent and antifusionist candidate suffered the consequences.[20]

A new issue, prohibition, gained greater prominence in the 1880s and generated a popular movement in Texas. Prohibitionists asked the legislature to present to the voters a constitutional amendment banning alcohol. Throughout the late 1870s and early 1880s, prohibition advocates had failed to obtain their goals but succeeded in causing controversy. In 1882 the Greenback Party criticized Democrats for trying to ignore the issue. Many Democratic politicians realized prohibition could be very divisive and sought to avoid it entirely. Others, like J. B. Cranfill, editor of the *Gatesville Advance,* joined the prohibition movement. Cranfill organized prohibition state conventions in 1884 and again in 1886. Although mildly criticizing Republicans, he saved his most intense criticism for fellow Democrats who had the power to make prohibition a reality. As the issue grew in influence, the Democratic Party split into factions. Powerful Democrats such as Congressman Roger Q. Mills and Gov. Lawrence Sullivan Ross opposed prohibition, while Sen. Sam Bell Maxey and Congressman John H. Reagan favored the idea.[21]

Publicly, Cuney said turmoil in the Democratic Party over prohibition "was having no effect" on the Republican Party. When asked if the disgruntled Democrats might switch parties, Cuney responded: "They have nowhere to go, as they, are primarily Democrats, and secondarily, Prohibitionists. Should the Democratic party in its convention next year declare prohibition undemocratic, it will be offensive to many prohibition Democrats, but they will not, for that reason, join the Republican party; but would become out and out prohibitionists were it not for the fear, on their part, that it might in some way aid the Republican party, which to their minds, is a greater evil than whiskey."[22]

Privately, Cuney delighted in the internal dissension taking place in the Democratic Party. He also considered any tactical advantage Republicans might achieve and the moral dilemma of prohibition itself. "I have been waiting and watching developments on this question—hoping to see some way by which the Republican party in this state could reap political advantage out of it. I've noticed that many of the big guns of Democracy are squirming and dodging trying to evade the issue. . . . [Prohibitionists] keep insisting that it is a moral and not a political question, [but] as all questions that require the political machinery of the people is a political question, and only moral insofar as all Legislation tends in that direction. While I recognize the great evil growing out of the excessive use of liquor yet I do not believe that prohibition will prohibit."[23]

Cuney wanted to play it safe but noted, "With the Priesthood on the one side and the activity of the Liquor dealers on the other it has assumed a rather unpleasant aspect for me." When the Dallas Anti-Prohibition Convention asked Cuney to serve on its executive committee, he refused. A statement of support either way might harm future fusion possibilities, so Cuney decided to keep his views on prohibition to himself. The prohibition amendment ended in a "slim" defeat at the polls, with Republicans, especially Germans, voting solidly against it, while the Democrats split. Democratic factionalism on the issue continued to heat up. Antiprohibition elements at the 1888 Democratic state convention tried to make their stance synonymous with loyalty to the party.

Appeals for general unity won the day, but the party loyalty of many prohibitionists appeared strained.[24]

Black Republicans faced a more formidable problem than prohibition: disfranchisement. Following Reconstruction, white intimidation and violence against black Texans continued but not with the same intensity. In the mid-1880s, Democratic Vigilance and Protection organizations began to form in greater numbers, especially where large populations of African Americans resided. Efforts to disfranchise black voters became increasingly violent. One such incident took place in Washington County. Two years earlier, someone had gunned down three black election officials while they counted votes. Black Republicans decided not to let that happen in 1886. When whites again tried to interfere with the electoral process, black election officials fought back, killing the son of a prominent Democrat. Whites overpowered and arrested three blacks. Afterward, Democrats wasted no time in stirring up racial hatred. A large mob organized, dragged the prisoners from their Brenham cells, and lynched all three.[25]

Cuney and other outraged African Americans called a meeting to protest. They condemned the violence and criticized the governor's double standard in "sending troops to quell imaginary Negro uprisings" while doing nothing to stop white mobs from lynching blacks. Cuney's actions in leading the protest and speaking out against the "cowardly mob" increased his usual number of death threats. In a trip to Austin shortly after the incident, Cuney made a point of stopping in Brenham to consult with friends. He ignored threats against his life, contemptuously dismissing possible perpetrators as "cowards." In a subsequent investigation by the U.S. Senate, Democrats denied that violence against blacks took place. Sen. Richard Coke of Texas denied antiblack violence occurred and claimed Democrats were the real victims.[26]

Despite continued white hostility, black Texans maintained leadership in several successful communities. The more successful the community became, however, the more hostile the white reaction. Politically and financially successful African Americans, over whom whites had little control, became the focal point of their hostility. Fort Bend County in the mid-1880s represented one such success story. The black population outnumbered whites four to one. Many blacks owned prosperous farms and businesses; some even became wealthy. During and after Reconstruction, black Republicans ran for and won elected offices. Black offi-

cials from the tax accessor to the state senator served the county well
with no clear-cut examples of corruption or abuse of power. Some whites,
including ex-Confederates, cooperated with black officeholders. Cuney
had many close friends and allies within the black community.[27]

Democrats in Fort Bend County decided to subvert the will of the
majority. In 1888 young whites formed the Young Men's Democratic Club.
The "Jaybirds," as the club became known, fielded its first slate of candidates in 1888. Republicans, now called "Woodpeckers," attempted to
hold on to power with an all-white slate. At first the Jaybirds employed
intimidation against black voters. The tactic backfired when a Jaybird
sympathizer, J. M. Shamblin, refused to allow "political agitators" on
his plantation to intimidate his black workers. Some unknown assailant
murdered Shamblin and wounded another white man shortly afterward.
On September 5, Jaybirds met at the courthouse, drew up a list of seven
African Americans, and ordered them to immediately leave the county.
County Clerk Charles M. Ferguson and teacher James D. Davis, both
Cuney friends and fellow Masons, were among those forced to leave.

When, in the fall elections, the Jaybirds failed to win at the polls, the
county swiftly disintegrated into mob violence. Eventually, Gov. Sul Ross
sent in the state militia. Though he may have wanted to restore order,
which was the official reason for calling out the troops, he also wanted to
see Democrats in charge in Fort Bend. The governor assigned his adjutant general the task of restoring order and reorganizing the county. When
the adjutant general left the county, the Jaybird faction was in complete
control. Upon leaving, he reportedly stated, "the next time he came back
he would not come as an official but would come back to help kill every
Negro in the county."[28]

Cuney considered the Fort Bend incident both an outrage and a tragedy. With each new violent act, black Republican strength diminished.
But Cuney refused to sit back and watch the party disintegrate. He helped
Ferguson sue under the Civil Right Act of 1875 in U.S. Circuit Court. He
wrote letters to black Masonic Lodges across the country requesting "an
assessment of five dollars per lodge" to finance the lawsuit. In a letter to
Assistant Secretary of the Treasury George Tichenor, Cuney proposed
"to make a test case of this suit, as to whether a man can be driven from
his home and his property, by the oligarchy which not only now rules the
South, but proposes to rule the country—because he dares to differ with
it on political issues." He criticized northerners for being "asleep on this

Southern question. . . . The South has ceased to be a democracy so far as the Negro is concerned." After a federal grand jury in Galveston indicted sixty-two white perpetrators in Fort Bend, they settled the case out of court.[29]

At the county and state conventions, Cuney continued to vent his anger, drawing the ire of Democrats. At the Galveston County Convention, he accused Democrats of being "wholly at fault" for violence in Fort Bend and Washington Counties. Democratic newspapers accused Cuney of "rabid partisanship." Some charged that he was giving "Northern Republicans the impression that Negroes were not safe in the South." Others accused him of making inflammatory speeches "that incites Negroes when in the majority to dominate over their white neighbors until the latter rise and either precipitate bloodshed or force them to leave." Many white Republicans agreed with Democratic attacks on Cuney and may have sympathized with the antiblack violence. Cuney promised that those Republicans "who were so solicitous about the *good name* of Texas when some of us dared to denounce the outrages" would not "hold again the places of honor and profit in Texas."[30]

Cuney reacted to the outrages on several levels: as a black man who sought to protect his race, as a politician who sought to protect his political base, and as a concerned citizen on an intellectual level. Before being abruptly ended by the Civil War, Cuney's northern schooling had taught him the basics of a classical education. After the war he continued his education through his own means. He had become well versed in "Hebrew, Greek, and Roman History." From his understanding of history, Cuney intellectualized his own political philosophy and applied it to political circumstances. He knew that other democracies often drifted "into oligarchies and then become monarchies." "In a large part of the South oligarchical governments now prevail," and those "who have the courage of their convictions, and are true to the fundamental principles of democracy must stand firm and combat the further encroachments of the hydroheaded monster." It was clear to Cuney that the southern oligarchies had allowed "the growth of a brute force which overrides law and order and settles by lynch law and mob violence those questions which ought to be settled by the Courts of the land."[31]

While lesser politicians might have become disheartened by white attempts to disfranchised black voters, Cuney continued his efforts to keep African Americans in the political process. Party leadership during this period was not for the faint of heart. State and county conventions in nineteenth-century Texas tended to be raucous affairs, with fistfights and occasional gunplay common occurrences. Cuney's personal leadership style tended to be very aggressive before victory and conciliatory afterward. He used invective, humor, and praise in equal measure. Opponents seldom gave as good as they received but were nonetheless aggressive in their attacks. Cuney's adherents remained very loyal and seldom failed to weigh in on his side. His enemies seldom failed to do the opposite. He often let conventions get out of hand until called on to calm things down. Although Cuney took an active interest in establishing convention ground rules, he often ignored those rules once conventions got under way. As "party boss," Cuney used tactics commonly used by other nineteenth-century political bosses.

The 1888 Galveston County Convention provides an excellent example of Cuney's leadership style. On an unusually cold April night in Galveston, two hundred Republicans met in a black Baptist church on Avenue L. The night before the convention, precincts held primaries to select delegates to the county convention according to the rules established at the state convention in 1886. Evidently, Cuney did not like the outcome. Ed Davis, handpicked by Cuney as chairman of the County Executive Committee, called the convention to order and announced it would be a "Republican mass meeting." Further, "the delegates elected the night previous at the primaries would not constitute the personnel of the convention, but would be entitled to vote just as any other citizen." To anyone who might oppose this action, he warned, "the convention would in all likelihood sit down upon them." Davis, who carried a heavy cane he used as a gavel and that was "convenient in most any emergency," simply ruled the opposition out of order.[32]

Cuney personally nominated his choices for convention officials and then chose the "tellers" who would count the vote. Cuney nominated Davis as permanent chairman, and his opponents nominated "Louis Johnson, colored, as chairman." When Cuney named two old friends to count the vote, the "anti-Cuney" forces began "a general rush toward the stage." Spectators began looking "for a way out." No sooner was order restored and the vote taken than another incident led to "pandemonium and bedlam." At that point Cuney took over the meeting. He garnered laughs from the audience when he called one opponent "a disreputable thief and scoundrel, and one who would sell Christ." The *Galveston Daily*

News reported: "His remarks were elegant, aggressive, and forcible, and just such a speech as fits just such an emergency. His abuse of those who stood in front of him, known as his opponents, was terrific. His remarks were also tempered with a good deal of self-laudation. He had no ambition except to serve the public good. He asked no quarters, and would give none."[33]

Black Republicans continued to face disfranchisement efforts by Democrats as Cuney's prestige and prominence within the national party and in Texas grew. Cuney began 1888 hoping his old friend James G. Blaine would win the presidency. In early April Republicans met to select delegates-at-large to the national convention. Cuney told the convention, "Blaine bore the banner in defeat; he will carry it aloft in victory." He maintained a tight reign on the convention, hoping to keep controversy to a minimum while controlling the selection process. Although his white adversaries favored John Sherman for president, they appeared less vocal than at previous meetings. Besides Cuney, Charles Ferguson, J. B. Rector, and Webster Flanagan, all allies, received delegate positions. In an apparent conciliatory move toward whites, Cuney allowed Convention Chairman A. M. Cochran, the 1884 gubernatorial nominee, to name the four alternates. Though most of the delegates appeared to support Blaine for president, the convention did not instruct delegates who to vote for at the national convention.[34]

Plagued by gout and many other ailments real and imagined, Blaine did not seek the presidency in 1888. By the time the national convention rolled around, support for the "Plumed Knight" among the Texas delegation and nationally appeared waning. Blaine wrote a friend that the nomination of Benjamin Harrison from Indiana would be "the best and wisest that we could make." Once the convention got under way, supporters such as Cuney and James Clarkson tried to keep a Blaine candidacy viable. Blaine kept hopes alive by not declaring unequivocally he was not a candidate. Most believed he would accept the nomination if drafted. If Blaine would not run, Cuney's close friend James Clarkson favored Iowa's William Allison, but many considered John Sherman the front-runner. Cuney disliked Sherman, who had years earlier dismissed him from his customs position. When Blaine finally removed his name from consideration and support for Allison failed to materialize, Clarkson led the movement toward the "Dark Horse" Benjamin Harrison.[35]

Cuney, an eternal optimist, returned to Texas convinced Harrison would win the presidency. He knew Republicans would not carry Texas but hoped for a good showing. Democrats, he believed, would lose nationally because of the tariff issue. He thought they would "try to appeal to both sides on the tariff question with a double ender on the next national platform . . . [and] say to manufacturing interests that it means protection, and say to the rural and shipping interests that it means free trade." Cleveland, he thought, would try to satisfy both sides. Protectionism constituted a basic tenet of Republican philosophy that Cuney fully supported. He hoped high tariffs would eventually spur an industrial base in the South in which black labor could play an important part.[36]

The harmony of the 1886 state convention did not continue in 1888. White Republicans, who began to organize their own clubs in 1884, directly challenged Cuney for leadership once again. He contemptuously referred to his opponents as "Lily Republicans" and "Lily Whites." In two words Cuney had identified a movement, its goals, and philosophy. Albion Tourgee thought the designation appropriate, "for as everybody knows, that faction thus arrogating to itself purity, capacity and patriotism, is organized for plunder." Lily-white plunder revolved around patronage that they believed rightfully belonged to them should Republicans return to the White House. They hoped to weaken or at least embarrass Cuney by placing a nominee in the governor's race. Cuney pushed through a fusion effort with independent candidate Marion Martin, hoping to attract votes for Harrison. Martin, the candidate of the Prohibition Party, also received the endorsement of the newly formed Union Labor Party. Many Lily Whites openly supported Democrat Sul Ross for governor.[37]

Harrison proved to be an excellent candidate. Together with Matthew Quay, chairman of the Republican National Committee, Harrison rejected a "bloody shirt" campaign in favor of "an orderly campaign of education, featuring pamphlets and broadsides to be sent all over the country." On his front porch he received ninety-four different delegations, tailor-made his speeches to suit those present, had aides edit each speech, and afterward distributed them to newspapers. He followed four themes: tariff protection, benefits for veterans, sound currency, and nationalism. While the popular vote was one of the closest in American history, Harrison easily gained enough electoral votes to defeat Grover Cleveland.[38]

The election of Harrison represented a turning point in Cuney's career as important as the death of Edmund Davis. Since Davis's death,

Wright Cuney had defeated his old enemy A. G. Malloy and other white Republican officeholders who had opposed his leadership. In doing so Cuney solidified his black support; indeed, black Republican loyalty made his rise possible. Through his Masonic activities, Cuney had created a network of important black contacts throughout the state. As a spokesman for African Americans both in and out of the party, Cuney decried the events at Fort Bend and other violent Democratic attempts to disfranchise black voters.

Some historians have written that Cuney focused too much on climbing the ladder to the top and that he did not adequately represent the interest of other African Americans. Another criticism has argued that Cuney did not do enough in the area of civil rights. Yet his public statements and actions show a man dedicated to both equality and civil rights.

Cuney also proved himself a practical politician. He knew that whites far outnumbered blacks in Texas and that he could not afford to alienate his white friends and supporters. Cuney's fusion efforts also reflected this practical approach. Fusion allowed the Republican Party to remain a prominent influence in Texas politics. Cuney had no illusions about politics or what it would take for him to succeed. In many ways his tactics at county and state conventions appeared heavy handed, though no more so than the tactics of his opponents. His white opponents sought to ignore the black Republican majority and maintain their positions by keeping blacks out of leadership roles. Cuney also had personal ambitions. With a Republican in the White House, he looked forward to strengthening the Republican Party through the power of patronage. Cuney also had his eye on the collector of customs office for Galveston, which could make him the most important black officeholder in the South.

CHAPTER 5

Party and Patronage

"WE CANNOT HOPE TO MAINTAIN OUR INTEGRITY, as we all who love our country would wish to do, by evading our honest obligations." Wright Cuney made this statement in his last speech before a Republican state convention. He referred to the obligations of government and men to meet their responsibilities in government and in life. Cuney died just months afterward, with his integrity intact. For fourteen years he had ably led his party. A man of immense political talents, Cuney believed he had an obligation to protect the political rights of other African Americans. He also loved politics and the give and take involved in the political process. Had Cuney not been black, he might have won election to a high office. While his skin color precluded elective position, the inauguration of Benjamin Harrison as president gave him an opportunity to secure the appointment of collector of customs at Galveston. No other African American would achieve such an important domestic appointment in the late-nineteenth-century South. As the last decade of his life revealed, Cuney continued to face immense political challenges both from within his own party and from outside. When he chose to support a loyal friend, William Allison, for the 1896 Republican presidential nomination over William McKinley, Cuney's opponents forced him out of the party leadership. Until that time he had repelled white attacks while maintaining the African American role in the Republican Party.[1]

Following Harrison's election, Lily Whites feared Cuney would become more powerful and influential then ever before. They began to form their local white clubs into a statewide organization. The Lily White plan of organization left little doubt about their objectives, "A reorganization of the party in this State, upon a basis removing the elements now operating to its prejudice and injury." Although African Americans represented 90 percent of Republican voters, Lily Whites proposed a division "giving each race political representation upon an equitable basis." They argued this would actually protect African Americans because "the fear of Negro domination in the South has led to practices which in many localities, have deprived that race of the constitutional right of suffrage, and which, if continued, will prove fatal to our Republican form of government." One Lily White leader put it more clearly: "No sane white man will claim a Negro as his equal, no matter what party he may affiliate with."[2]

Cuney, for the time being, saw the Lily Whites as an irritation but not a threat. Cuney and friends reveled in Harrison's victory. His ally James Clarkson became vice chairman of the Republican National Committee and was designated to become first assistant postmaster general. Cuney suddenly found himself the center of attention, besieged by newspaper reporters, and drowning in letters from office seekers. What would happen to political patronage in the state? Would Cuney seek the customs collectorship at Galveston? Who would he recommend for positions? What would happen to those appointed by Cleveland? For Cuney, these and other questions would have to wait. He wrote to a friend: "I am deluged with letters of request for this or that and everything else; but under the circumstances I am compelled to withhold my endorsement. The woods are full of place hunters and how they will be satisfied is a problem that, to me, at present is unsolvable."[3]

Cuney wanted very much the appointment as collector of customs. He also knew the position would give him greater control over patronage. If he did not receive the post, many would see it as a sign of weakness and a personal slight, putting his leadership of the party in jeopardy. Black Republicans viewed a possible Cuney appointment as a reward for their sacrifices and loyalty to the party. The campaign for Cuney's appointment began immediately after the election. He received support from several important sources. In December, 1888, the Democratic *Galveston Daily News* ran an editorial acknowledging that since a Republican would be appointed collector, "No Republican in Galveston is more entitled to consideration than N. W. Cuney, and it is supposed that he will be a power in the distribution of political patronage." Galveston's business and civic leaders also began preparing citizen petitions recommending Cuney for the Collectors Office.[4]

Because of mixed signals coming out of Washington following Harrison's inauguration, the appointment of Cuney appeared far from certain. Anxiety existed among southern blacks concerning the president's attitudes toward civil rights and patronage issues. During the campaign, Harrison stressed a strong commitment to a "free and honest popular ballot, and the just and equal representation of all the people." Once Harrison assumed office, however, contradictory messages began coming out of Washington about his intentions toward African Americans. His statement promising to "make no appointment of colored persons to office simply by way of recognizing them as a race" did nothing to ease their fears. With feelings of abandonment at the hands of his predecessors still fresh in their minds, southern blacks wanted recognition through patronage. As months passed and few African Americans received appointments, *The New York Times* wrote, "notwithstanding the fact they do nearly all the Republican voting, they are ignored and their white allies get all the offices, they are mad and disgusted and swear that they will not vote the Republican ticket any longer."[5]

Opposition to Cuney came not from Democrats but from Lily White Republicans. One wrote Harrison that Cuney was "one of the worst gamblers and whisky men in the county, [and] controls the colored vote in the interest of the Democratic party." Another believed "no southern man of respectability will accept a subordinate position under a Negro collector," but he added Cuney might make a "credible" representative to Liberia. Most opposition came from Lily White organizations with a long laundry list of complaints. The Central Republican League Club of Harris County called a special meeting and presented the president with a signed petition: "For years past political preferment has been obtained in state politics generally by combination only with or serving the wishes of one N. W. Cuney, and in local politics the highest bidder has controlled the situation with local leaders. The skill of Mr. Cuney as a politician has secured him leadership of the colored Republicans, and his political enmity is so feared that men with political aspirations dare not, as we are informed and believe, enter the list of announced candidates for the Collectorship of the Port of Galveston, though the almost universal private sentiment of all Republicans interested in having the true interest of the party served are against his appointment."[6]

Despite Lily White opposition, Cuney's long list of endorsements far outweighed negative statements. Besides the expected recommendations from political friends and supporters, endorsements from Galveston citizens, merchants, and civic leaders topped the list. Many mentioned his "honesty and personal integrity," some his support for education, and others his prominence in the community. The few existing Republican newspapers in Texas generally praised Cuney for his "unimpeachable Republicanism." Many African American recommendations expressed a general sense of pride in his accomplishments. Harrison's close friend and schoolmate Edwin H. Terrell, who became ambassador to Belgium, strongly recommended Cuney for "his industry, capacity, and personal integrity." J. N. Sawyer, president of Mallory Steamship Lines and who cooperated with Cuney over Galveston's labor troubles, believed him to be a man "without taint or stain." Galveston's mayor, Democrat R. L. Fulton, listed Cuney's long list of accomplishments as alderman and head of the "Water Commission." In his last term as alderman, noted Fulton, "he was elected by the city at large—a rare compliment to a Republican, by a city with nearly a three thousand Democratic majority."[7]

For the first eighteen months of his administration, Harrison spent four to six hours daily making appointment decisions; 60 percent of his mail concerned patronage. To the dismay of powerful congressmen, he had a reputation for asking their advice and then ignoring it. Still, Republican leaders gave their advice. Some northern Republicans, including James G. Blaine according to some reports, advised Harrison against putting "a Negro in the chief Federal Office in Texas." Many considered Cuney a "civil rights Nigger" and a troublemaker. Even with advice to the contrary, Harrison began to change his policy. He appointed several "old Negro Leaders" such as Frederick Douglass, Blanche K. Bruce, and Robert Smalls and also began to consider younger African Americans. By July, many influential black leaders began to view Harrison in a more favorable light.[8]

Clarkson's position as vice chairman of the party and assistant postmaster gave him enormous power over patronage. He filled over fifty-five thousand postmaster positions in less than two years. He made the appointment of Cuney to the collectorship one of his foremost concerns. In July Cuney went to Washington to try and assure his appointment. Clarkson personally escorted Cuney for an early morning meeting with the president. The wily Clarkson probably had advance notice because they arrived at the very time Harrison and Treasury Secretary Windom were making their decision concerning the Galveston post. Clarkson went to see the president first. According to Clarkson, Harrison had just written down someone other than Cuney for the position. He told the president that was incorrect and reminded him of their decision for Cuney. Harrison asked, "If you were President would you give the most important position in Texas and one of the most important in the whole South, to a Negro?" "Yes, and be glad of the chance, when so worthy and fit a man for the position, and a colored man endorsed as to fitness and reliability for the place by all the Democratic business men of the city, could be found," Clarkson replied. Harrison then wrote Cuney's name instead.[9]

Reaction to Cuney's appointment came swiftly. *The New York Times* editorialized, "If President Harrison wants to win votes from white Democrats of Texas he could hardly have set about it in a worse way than making the appointment today of N. Wright Cuney to be Collector of Customs at Galveston." T. Thomas Fortune of the *New York Age* took the opposite tack: "Let the good work proceed. Turn the Southern Democratic rascals out." Most Texas newspapers took for granted Cuney would be the next collector, and few expressed surprise. Texas Democratic senator Reagan announced his support as did Senator Coke. "I have no objection to Cuney, save his color," Coke announced. Rarely did the U.S. Senate turn down presidential appointments in the nineteenth century, and Cuney's was no exception; he received quick confirmation.[10]

Cuney returned home to another hero's welcome. He accomplished a feat against great odds that just a few years earlier seemed unthinkable. In Texas, and arguably the entire South, Cuney had received the most important federal domestic position any African American would obtain for the remainder of the century. The worst fears of Lily Whites had become a reality. Many feared Cuney would control all federal patronage. An unofficial compromise appeared to develop with some North Texas whites that allowed them to recommend justice and revenue appointments, but it is doubtful this was possible without Cuney's acquiescence. A compromise adhered to Cuney's political philosophy of conciliation after victory, but this time there were limits. Judging by his recommendations and confirmations, the compromise did not extend beyond northern Texas. In western Texas, the only other exception, Cuney followed the wishes and advice of E. H. Terrell, who had become a close friend.[11]

But there was no compromise concerning the Lily Whites. Cuney would fight tooth and nail to preclude as many of their appointments as possible. The name of James P. Newcomb rested at the top of the list for elimination. Newcomb, the most famous of the Lily White leaders, desperately wanted the postmastership of San Antonio, his hometown and political base. He made numerous trips to Washington to lobby for it. Newcomb had the support of many in San Antonio's civic and business community, who deluged Clarkson and the president with letters. Clarkson simply ignored the request, asked whom Cuney wanted, and appointed his choice.[12]

The black Texan walked a fine line. Cuney wanted to reward his "race" and his political friends, but because of his skin color, he knew Washington and the public would scrutinize his actions more than any other official. He went to great lengths to appoint qualified people to positions. Cuney wrote Terrell, "It shall be my highest ambition to vindicate the confidence of my friends in recommending and to justify the wisdom of the administration in making this appointment." To an office seeker who offered to pay for his endorsement, Cuney tactfully responded that not "all public men demand and expect pay from whom they endorse for pubic office." Yet he did not shy away from partisanship. "It is my duty to support those, for place, of my party faith who are fitted to discharge the duties of offices to which they are appointed."[13]

Cuney repeatedly stressed his opposition to any color line, white or black. He could not afford to do otherwise but stressed that blacks would have to receive their fair share of positions. In watching out for the "welfare of my people," Cuney promised to promote "Negroes to the place and position they deserve." Beside his own appointments, Cuney urged other officeholders to recommend qualified blacks. He chastised any black official who did not follow his example. To a black supervisor of the census, Cuney wrote: "There is a large number of young men . . . who have made applications in the several districts whom I know to be thoroughly fit and competent in every way. . . . And I can not see how a representative of the federal government under a Republican administration can afford to discriminate against them on account of color."[14]

The years from 1889 through 1892 became happy and successful ones for Cuney and his family. He received recognition from the administration and national Republicans for his efficient management of the Collectors Office. He supervised the building of a new and modern customhouse. When the Republican National Committee met in November, 1891, to select a sight for the next convention, it chose Cuney as the presiding officer. Cuney maintained his position in the community through his continued involvement in civic affairs. His family celebrated with pride the enrollment of his daughter, Maud, in the prestigious New England Conservatory of Music. His son, Garrison, would soon set off for Tillotson College in Austin. Although Adelina Cuney continued to fight the ravages of tuberculosis, her health seemed to be improving after several trips to health spas. But amid success Cuney met a few setbacks and fought many battles.[15]

Continued scenes of black and white conflict dominated conventions. African Americans went into the state convention in 1890 overconfident of their success. "We have got dem white folks where de hair is short," one black delegate exclaimed. Cuney entered the convention hoping for a more harmonious relationship with whites and moved toward conciliation. Overconfidence seems to have clouded Cuney's judgment too. He decided not to interfere directly in the selection of candidates.

For their part, the Lily Whites tried a new tactic—divide and conquer. The shrewd and politically savvy James Newcomb, publisher of the new newspaper *The White Republican*, appeared to be the unofficial leader of Lily White opposition. His newspaper expressed the desire of whites to protect black civil rights. Lily Whites nominated Webster Flanagan for governor, a man well liked by most blacks and whites and at various times a Cuney supporter. Someone nominated Charles W. Ogden in opposition, the party leader's old friend and supporter. Cuney did not interject himself in the voting. By a fifty-seven-vote majority, Flanagan won the day. Many newspapers wrote that it represented a defeat for Cuney. Democrat James Hogg easily beat Flanagan in the fall election.[16]

The year 1890 began with hopeful signs coming out of Washington for southern blacks. Sen. Henry Cabot Lodge, a longtime advocate of a free ballot and black civil rights, introduced legislation providing for federal supervision of congressional races. Fearful southern whites knew to whom the bill was directed and labeled it the "Force Bill." Harrison, a strong advocate of the Fifteenth Amendment, favored the legislation. Besides, administration leaders had given up the idea of making southern whites into Republicans and felt they had nothing to lose. Cuney and the Texas party endorsed the bill at their 1890 convention. Lily Whites, not surprisingly, condemned the measure as unnecessary. The legislation continued to play a controversial role in Texas politics.[17]

After 1890, Cuney never again let his guard down in party politics. He believed 1892 was shaping up to be a very interesting year in Texas. Nationally, he hoped for Harrison's reelection but knew if Cleveland won the Democratic nomination, it would be a tough campaign. Cuney could see an exciting political battle on the way and thought "Republicans would have to use our wisest political judgment to arrive at what is best to do." He wanted to wait until the state convention so he could "consult with others . . . to decide what would be the greatest good for the party." He warned Republicans, "no sulking or treachery in our ranks." Cuney also worried about the growing volatility in the political climate.[18]

The developing Populist movement became a special concern that year. Cuney had a new rival on the scene who challenged the Republican boss for the hearts and minds of black voters. John B. Rayner convinced Populist leaders that black voters would be essential to their party's success. He had much in common with Cuney. Born a slave in 1850, he was the mulatto son of Kenneth Rayner, a famous North Carolina politician and plantation owner. Like Cuney, Rayner received from his father an education and a love for politics. He held a number of low-level elected positions in North Carolina before moving to Texas in 1880. After an involvement in the 1887 Prohibition campaign, Rayner joined the Populist Party in 1892. Evidently, Rayner developed a great dislike for Cuney, and even many black Republicans, calling them "hotel flunkies, barbers, dude school teachers, ignorant preachers, [and] saloon waiters." Rayner failed in his recruitment efforts, however, as most black Republicans remained loyal to their Republican leader.[19]

At the Republican State Convention in March, 1892, Cuney kept a tight reign on the proceedings. No conciliation efforts with Lily Whites were made at this meeting. As far as Cuney was concerned, Lily Whites did not exist. Ignored and defeated at the state convention, they again called a separate convention at which they passed a resolution against the Lodge bill and nominated A. J. Houston, one Sam Houston's sons, for governor. Later at the national convention, Lily Whites contested the seating of Cuney's delegation. The Credentials Committee not only unanimously voted against the Lily Whites but also stated they "represented a political organization in Texas which is un-American and un-Republican." Harrison won renomination. Cuney returned to Texas at the height of his political power.[20]

In early February, 1892, the *Dallas Morning News* asked Cuney what he thought would happen in the Democratic Party that year. "I think Mr. Hogg will be renominated. . . . He will be elected unless there is a bolt. . . . If the opponents of the Governor have the courage of their convictions, and are not afraid of the old slogan of Democracy, Edmund Davis and Negro domination, there will be a bolt." Cuney also thought the "great mass" of Republicans would vote for the bolters "in order to save the state from the effects of the reckless class legislation of the present administration." Cuney's prediction came true. The Democrats became embroiled in a messy fight between two popular Texas figures. Hogg, the incumbent governor and reformer who established the Texas Railroad Commission, against George Clark, a prominent railroad attorney and leader of the antiprohibition movement. After Hogg won renomination, Clark Democrats bolted the convention to nominate their man for the fall election.[21]

Publicly, Cuney left little doubt which way he leaned, writing to a friend: "It is for the best interest of Texas to beat Mr. Hogg. . . . Mr. Clark has allied himself with the best brains and character in the state . . . , Which will enable the state to escape further dry rot." Even though whites attended in large numbers, Cuney dominated the Republican State Convention in September as never before. If anyone doubted the outcome of the voting, that doubt was dispelled when J. L. "Sin Killer" Griffin, a black revivalist and Cuney friend, ended the convention's opening prayer with "Oh, Lord, bless George Clark." The seemingly impossible became a reality. Black Republicans and their white allies would join forces with conservative Democrats to oppose a reformist governor.[22]

Cuney pursued this course for a number of reasons. Foremost, he hated the Democratic Party. If Clark won with black support, the Democratic Party in Texas might be split for years to come. Ideologically, Cuney's Republican ideas coincided with many of Clark's conservative ideas; he even praised Clark as a man of "Republican principals." Both men opposed the Railroad Commission. Cuney did so because it interfered with his Republican probusiness philosophy and he believed regulation was just one step away from "government ownership of railroads." Clark also voiced some of the same concerns accusing Hogg of driving investment capital from Texas. According to Cuney, Hogg's "principles seek to undermine our whole system of business which has existed for years, and under which our country has become great and strong, and made itself the foremost among the nations of the world."[23]

A Clark victory, won with black support, would certainly upset the racial hierarchy and might put an end to the efforts of some Democrats to disfranchise black voters. To Hogg's credit, he spoke out against the "Lynch Law," which led to dozens of black deaths in Texas every year, but Cuney doubted his sincerity. Eventually, the governor urged passage of an antilynching bill but did little to stop it as the number of blacks lynched increased yearly. Also, the legislature in 1890 passed, and Hogg signed, the first Jim Crow law separating black and white accommodations on railroads. Cuney also disliked what he called the "ridiculous isms." For Cuney, "Hoggism" and "Populism" represented a two-sided coin of "socialism and communism." He saw little difference between Hogg and the Populist nominee, Thomas L. Nugent.[24]

The election of 1892 became one of the most memorable in Texas history. In the highly charged political atmosphere produced by Cuney's endorsement of Clark, Democrats pulled out the race card whenever possible. Senator Coke coined the phrase "Three C's—Clark, Cuney, and the Coons," and the Democrats used it throughout the state. Hogg supporters distributed offensive racial cartoons and poems linking Clark and Cuney. The campaign brought out the old sawhorse about black domination and tied the Lodge election bill to such fears. For his part, Hogg rarely made racial attacks and chose to take the high road, while his associates did the race baiting. At the same time, his campaign made efforts to attract the black vote, building on Hogg's antilynching rhetoric. He hired black speakers to campaign in African American districts and formed black Hogg clubs wherever possible. The governor used his power over state patronage to counterbalance the federal patronage controlled by Cuney. His campaign also used "the time tested Democratic methods of bribery, intimidation, and overt violence."[25]

Cuney campaigned across the state for Clark and Harrison. In areas of large African American populations, Cuney began organizing "Negro Clark Clubs." To counter Hogg's appeals to black voters, he distributed circulars of Hogg's earlier statements concerning blacks. One quoted from an Austin speech in which, as attorney general, Hogg reportedly looked out over an audience of mostly black faces and stated, "I'll be damned that looks like the black map of Hell spread out before me." In a speech supporting the segregation of train cars, he reportedly stated, "the time had come when our wives and daughters should not ride in the same coach with flop eared negroes." Hogg did not deny or affirm that he made such statements, but if they hurt him among black voters, they helped solidify his white Democratic base.[26]

Many in the Hogg camp feared that the Cuney-Clark combination might win. With the backing of railroad and business interests, they knew Clark could outspend them. Most of Texas' major newspapers supported Clark, giving him a powerful outlet for his message. The Hogg campaign greatly feared that the Cuney Republicans would give Clark the votes needed to win a narrow victory. T. U. Lubbock thought Hogg could win but that Cuney would be a special problem, "for he will exert all of his power to carry out his deal with the Clarkites—He can be overcome; but it will take judicious management." In the end Cuney, Clark, and Nugent were overcome. Clark garnered a sizable 133,395 votes to Hogg's 190,486, with Nugent third.[27]

Harrison's defeat at the hands of Cleveland left Cuney with at least four more months in the Customs Office, depending on the speed of Cleveland's appointment process. If he had hopes of a relaxed and worry-free experience, they were soon dashed. Lily Whites hoped electoral defeat had weakened Cuney's position in the party and immediately began a campaign to discredit or at least embarrass him as collector. In petitions they charged him with "neglect of office" and with using "his prestige of office to interfere in local and national politics." They also took offense to Cuney's public statements referring to Lily Whites as "Fice dogs barking at his heels." After Cleveland's inauguration, Senator Coke used many of the same charges in lobbying for his immediate removal. At the same time, Galveston's mayor and businessmen petitioned the new president to keep this "able and faithful servant" in office until his replacement is confirmed by the Senate.[28]

In 1894 the Lily Whites took the offensive. They attempted to organize a fusion effort with the Populists on the congressional level, though without success. Then they floated the ruse of reconciliation by proposing a "census plan of representation." This plan, a forerunner to the all-white primary, proposed "to separate the races in primaries as they are in schools, churches, and railroads, and give to them a fixed and certain representation." Cuney rejected the idea, insisting that the Republican Party was one organization and any differences of opinion "will be adjusted in the convention hall." He pointed out the great disparity in the population, calling the plan unnecessary "because the whites have always out-numbered the Negroes in our state." Lily Whites had hoped to attract alienated black Republicans who had supported the Populist and Hogg campaigns, but they failed in that objective as these people rejoined the Republican Party.[29]

The Lily Whites tried to upstage Cuney and the regular organization by calling a separate convention prior to the official meeting in 1894 and nominated their own slate of candidates. Cuney remained in control at the regular convention, rejecting any fusion that year. The Lily White census plan, after some discussion, gained little support at the regular meeting. But trouble for Cuney could be seen on the horizon. His old friend Charles Ferguson, for whom Cuney had obtained federal employment after his time of troubles in Fort Bend County, turned against him. Charles and his brother Henry led the fight against Cuney's choice for state chairman, Dr. John Grant. Grant easily won, but the unexpected challenge gained the attention of the press, who labeled it a fight between the "Black and Tans." The defeat in 1892 and Populist recruitment of black voters began to take their toll on the Cuney Republicans. In the fall elections, the "People's party" surpassed the Republicans as Texas' second party. Though the party had declined in influence, Cuney remained its undisputed leader.[30]

In 1895 Cuney largely ignored his political concerns as his wife, Adelina, became increasingly ill with tuberculosis. The couple made numerous trips to health spas and to dryer climates, hoping to improve her condition, but to no avail. She died on October 29. Cuney was devastated by the death of "the promoter of his welfare and a counselor in his endeavors." According to daughter Maud, he never recovered from her passing, often suffering from depression. Her death and his depression also may have blurred his judgment about political affairs.[31]

During his wife's long illness, Cuney received several letters from Marcus Alonzo Hanna. Perhaps the first modern political operative, Hanna became the "genius" behind the campaign of William McKinley for president; since 1888, he had dedicated himself to the election of his old friend. McKinley and Hanna made a good political team. According to historian H. Wayne Morgan, "While McKinley could shake hands, make speeches, write courteous and thoughtful notes, and smile his way through conferences and receptions, he had a curious lack of talent for party organization work." The genius of Hanna derived from his organizational skills. He began McKinley's campaign by locking up the South. Southern states might vote Democratic, but southern Republicans did send delegations to national conventions.[32]

Hanna wanted Texas in the McKinley column. He anxiously wanted
to set up a meeting in New Orleans with Cuney, but the illness of Adelina
precluded him from going. Hanna then sent a special representative, Jim
Hill of Mississippi, to talk with Cuney personally. Hill tried but failed to
persuade Cuney to support McKinley for the 1896 Republican nomination. Undaunted, Hanna then wrote to Cuney: "I will say to you frankly
that I am very anxious to have you take charge of Gov. McKinley's interest in Texas, which I feel should soon receive some attention. I appreciate
that it is something of a task to fully perfect an organization and that
there would be expenses, etc., which no one should be asked to bear
alone. Then as to the proper men from whom to ask assistance in the
several Dist's—I will gladly co-operate in all this and write personal letters to those you may suggest—where you think it would have influence.
And in any other way do all I can to assist you, all contingent of course
upon your willingness in the matter."[33]

Hanna's letter and his desire to have Cuney direct the Texas campaign
for McKinley illustrated the respect shown Cuney by national Republican leaders. The attractive offer probably flattered and interested him
very much, but his loyalties lay elsewhere. Since early in his career, Cuney
had loyal and important personal and political friendships with James
Clarkson and William Allison. Only his loyalty to Blaine precluded Cuney
from supporting Allison in 1888. Now Allison hoped 1896 would be his
year. Clarkson, Allison's campaign manager, had long before lined up
Cuney for the effort. The Texan felt honor bound to support his old friends.
His loyalty would cost him dearly.[34]

On March 24, Republicans met to chose delegates to the national
convention. Unable to convince Cuney, Hanna enlisted the support of
Webster Flanagan. Especially worrisome for the Republican leader was
the loss to McKinley of John Grant, chosen by Cuney as chairman of the
state executive committee. For weeks prior to the meeting, rumors spread
that the McKinley men would try to oust Cuney. Going into the convention, Cuney formed an Allison-Reed alliance. Speaker of the House
Thomas Reed also contended for the nomination that year and had some
Texas support. Cuney felt confident about his convention prospects. The
night before, the *San Antonio Express* described Cuney as "smiling and
serene." He would later say, "The way to have peace is to fight for it."[35]

Shortly after the convention opened, Cuney announced he would personally challenge Grant for the convention chairmanship. He felt this
was essential to keep a McKinley delegation from going to the national

convention. Cuney's election seemed in doubt until a rumor spread through the delegations that "the white McKinleyites didn't want a d——d nigger to preside over the convention." Blacks immediately rallied around their leader, and his victory was assured. The announcement that Cuney won produced a long celebration by his supporters. He also controlled the selection process on the Credentials Committee. When Cuney announced the four men selected as delegates-at-large, the state delegates erupted in a riot. According to one newspaper: "Nature's weapons, bludgeons, bottles, pistols and knives all figured in it. Tables were smashed and chairs broken, while oaths and groans blended." The convention remained under the tight control of Cuney, despite loud and sometimes violent interruptions by McKinley's supporters. While Cuney won the day, the McKinley forces promised to contest the outcome at the national convention.[36]

Hanna had earned the respect of his Texas opponent. Cuney must have left for the St. Louis meeting unsure of the outcome not just for Allison but also for his own position. After participating in three successive national conventions and dozens of state and local conventions, he knew what happened to those on the losing side. Once in town, he surely realized that Allison's position was hopeless, but he stood by his loyal friend; Clarkson, his other old friend, could not attend the convention because of a severe illness. Under the efficient management of Mark Hanna and backed by a lot of money, McKinley had a lock on the convention before it started. True to their word, the McKinley forces contested the seating of Cuney's delegation. The Credentials Committee allowed the seating of ten McKinley delegates from the thirteen Texas congressional districts. Then the committee elected to place the seating of the two contesting groups of delegates-at-large before the convention as a whole. McKinley forces overwhelming controlled the convention, sealing Cuney's defeat. To add injury to insult, John Grant became the new national committeeman for Texas. Cuney lost his hold on leadership, not at the hands of the Lily Whites, but because he backed the wrong presidential candidate.[37]

Texas greeted Cuney's loss with shock, regret, and in many quarters relief. Because of his skin color, his "plucky" style, and personality, newspapers always knew they would have a good story. Some loved to hate and denigrate him, and a few fairly reported his views and exploits. In an evenhanded article, the *San Antonio Express* summed up his loss: "The entire Republican party of Texas was unable to cope with his energy, influence or generalship. It was only through an accident of politics that his enemies were able to call to their assistance the national leaders and dethrone, temporarily, at least the sable statesman. Viewed from a non-partisan standpoint, and without race prejudice, Cuney was entitled to a seat in the St. Louis convention. He had the Republican organization with him. Had there been nothing at stake for the McKinley managers in St. Louis, little reason would have been found why Cuney and his friends should not have been accorded the fruits of their labors. As it is, he is thrown out simply because of his fidelity to a minority candidate, and to make more room for the McKinley forces."[38]

Many believed that Cuney was only temporarily "dethroned." He did try to make a comeback at the Fort Worth state convention in September, running for temporary chairmanship but losing to Charles Ferguson. Cuney made his last speech at that meeting. He told the gathering to lay aside their differences and "secure the election of McKinley." Advising the new leadership, he implored that "brains and patriotism should run the party." Overall, he expressed his philosophy as a Republican and a public man, stating:

> Reputation is one thing, but character is pure gold, and on that you must judge a man, and that is the basis and the standard of what is right in life. . . .
>
> A man has no more right to trifle with his integrity than a woman has the right to trifle with her virtue. The best principle to lay down to people is to tell them to speak the truth; tell the people to be honest. Teach honesty and integrity to the people, and on that basis will this great American republic go on as she has been going, and continue to be the foremost nation on earth, and this we can do in our day and generation. And our children will learn to honor and respect it.[39]

Cuney left Fort Worth, exhausted and ill, to go to the dryer climate of San Antonio. Between then and the election, he made several trips, against the advice of his doctor, to campaign for McKinley. He attended numerous dinners held in his honor by different black organizations across the state. On a trip to Austin, Cuney contracted the flu, which was accompanied by seizures. He retired to Boerne, a health resort in southwestern

Texas, under the care of daughter Maud and a nurse. With the onslaught of winter, they returned to San Antonio. In January and February, 1897, his condition grew increasingly worse. His family, including his elderly mother, came down from Galveston. Early on March 3, he asked for his newspapers, read them, and gave Maud a memorandum to make sure the papers received "proper notification" of his death. Maud was at her father's side when he died and later wrote, "He Whispered, 'My work is ended'—a last farewell to the world and, drawing my face down to his, he kissed me good-bye."[40]

The Southern Pacific and the Santa Fe Railroads provided a private car to transfer the body from San Antonio to Galveston. The Texas adjutant general provided a guard of honor and the San Antonio black militia company escorted the casket. On March 6, three thousand people crowded into Galveston's Harmony Hall, with several thousand more outside, to hear the memorial ceremonies. Later that day, J. W. McKinney of Sherman officiated over Masonic services with Grand High Master Wilford H. Smith of New York giving the eulogy. With "hundreds lining the streets," a long funeral procession of mounted police, military companies, screwmen, longshoremen, and Masons accompanied the body to Lakeview Cemetery for burial.[41]

T. Thomas Fortune, a close friend and frequent house guest of Wright Cuney, wrote shortly after his death, "The devotion of the Afro-American race of Texas to Mr. Cuney was one of the strongest and strangest in our politics, and was such as no other man of his race has ever enjoyed in this country." Fortune was a keen observer of his era and of the South. He often criticized Southern black leaders for what he considered their timidity and acquiescence to whites. Cuney exemplified what Fortune believed black leaders had to do if African Americans were to reverse disfranchisement and segregation. He also acknowledged that Cuney was a special individual, "a natural leader and organizer of men."[42]

A critical analysis of Cuney's career points not only to many strengths but also to some weaknesses. Ideologically, Cuney followed the national Republican philosophy to the letter. In the Hogg-Clark governor's campaign, Cuney strongly opposed any form of business regulation, especially regulation of the railroads. In his fusion efforts with Populists, which he made for pragmatic reasons, Cuney opposed any easing of the money supply. In both instances, Cuney ignored the concerns of the African American tenant farmers and sharecroppers who made up a large portion of the Republican Party in Texas. Cuney appeared to have less under-standing of farm issues. Part of his attitude derives from his lack of power to do anything about rural problems. On another level Cuney represented the concerns of other middle-class black Republicans. He would have disagreed with such a characterization and probably would point with pride to his labor activities as evidence to the contrary. But even in that aspect, Cuney had to cooperate with business interests to fight the monopoly of the white unions. Because of their higher income when compared to most African Americans, the black dockworkers might be considered part of an emerging middle class.

Cuney found himself in a delicate situation as party leader. Even if he had wanted regulation or easier access to money, such positions might have cost him the support of his Republican friends in Washington. Cuney's strength lay in his considerable political accomplishments made in the face of a racially biased and hostile environment. He refused to sit back and be a pawn for white manipulation. Cuney fought back for his "race," for his party, and for himself. In the face of a repressive southern political system, Cuney had little effect on black Texans' daily lives; but in terms of racial pride and hopes for the future, his influence was substan-tial. As leader of the Republican Party, Cuney gave black Texans a trusted moral and political voice. Through his fusion efforts, he kept black Re-publicans in the political process. Cuney forced Democrats during the Jones and Clark campaigns to expend political capital to maintain their dominance. He loved the game of politics and thrived on political com-bat; Cuney knew how to play it well. In a racially prejudiced society in which whites considered blacks inferior, white politicians had to contend with a black man of superior qualities. Cuney passed along those quali-ties to his daughter, Maud. She would soon leave Texas to pursue her own career in music and the arts.

CHAPTER 6

Maud Cuney

Education and Marriage

SHORTLY AFTER HER DEATH in 1936, W. E. B. Du Bois wrote: "Maud Cuney was the bravest woman I have ever known. For those born in adversity, fighting fate becomes a habit, rather than a virtue; but when one is born to the purple and is first in mid-life overwhelmed by successive and relentless blows of every kind of cruelty and adversity, then to keep one's chin up, the eye unflinching, and the courage unfaltering, calls for the sort of soul men seldom see." Throughout her adult life, "Du," as Maud Cuney-Hare affectionately called him, remained her adviser and confidante. He perhaps knew her better than anyone else. Her correspondence with the famous black intellectual reveals an African American woman dedicated to music, literature, theater, and the "uplift" of her race. She continued to espouse her father's ideals and never backed down in the face of racism. Maud Cuney, who became known as Cuney-Hare by also using the name of her second husband, lived a remarkable life of success achieved by few African American women in the early twentieth century. A daughter of Texas and a woman of Boston, she triumphed despite immense obstacles and personal tragedy.[1]

Cuney-Hare belonged to a select group of early-twentieth-century African American professional women who succeeded outside the home. A graduate of the New England Conservatory of Music, she and baritone William Richardson gave concerts across the eastern seaboard, often with the accompaniment of Arthur Fiedler at the cello. She created the Allied Arts Centre in Boston, giving black youth and playwrights an outlet for their talents. Besides writing and directing her own plays, she wrote a biography of her famous father and edited a well-received book on poetry. Cuney-Hare traveled extensively to research the roots of black music and contributed articles on that subject to *The Crisis* magazine of the National Association for the Advancement of Colored People (NAACP), the *Christian Science Monitor,* and various other publications. Her most important written work, a book entitled *Negro Musicians and Their Music,* traces the development of black music from its African roots to the beginnings of jazz.

While producing this large body of writing, Cuney-Hare faced an unusual amount of personal tragedy. Both of her parents died of tuberculosis. She underwent a well-publicized and humiliating divorce from her first husband, losing custody of her daughter, Vera, in the process. Shortly after she regained custody, Vera died at age eight. In the Galveston hurricane of 1900, Cuney-Hare lost six members of her closely knit family, including her grandmother and her Uncle Nelson. Her brother, Lloyd, like her parents, contracted tuberculosis and became an invalid under her care. Her second husband and her mother-in-law suffered ill health throughout much of her marriage and also required her attention and care. Then in the early 1930s, doctors diagnosed Cuney-Hare with the cancer that eventually forced her to give up playing her beloved piano. Amazingly, under circumstances that might have limited a lesser person, Maud continued to persevere and succeed.

The first generation of African Americans born after slavery represents a fascinating and undeveloped aspect of historical scholarship. Among that generation, the children of educated mulatto parents became part of the black elite following Reconstruction. With the passage of Jim Crow laws, many of these young mulattoes left the South, seeking greater opportunities in the North. After migrating in the late 1890s and early 1900s, they joined the descendants of northern free blacks to form an influential black upper class. According to historian Willard B. Gatewood, "the overwhelming majority of aristocrats of color were indeed mixed-bloods ranging in color from light brown to 'yellow' to virtually white. Their appearance was obviously an advantage in a society that placed the highest premium on a white skin."[2]

African Americans of mixed heritage held an ambiguous position in both the black and white communities. The mere existence of mulattoes brought into question white ideas of "racial purity." Most northern whites adopted the southern one-drop rule toward mixed bloods and also considered mulattoes "intellectually superior" to darker-skinned individuals. Thus, whites believed, mixed heritage made mulattoes the natural leaders of other blacks. "On the negative side," writes Gatewood, "whites believed that mixed bloods were stirrers-up of strife, constantly demanding greater rights and privileges for themselves and awakening false aspirations among the black masses." Many whites also believed that mulattoes were "hybrids, morally weak, and physically degenerate." This led to the belief by many that mulattoes would eventually die out because of physical weakness.[3]

Attitudes toward lighter-skinned African Americans within the black community did not follow such clear-cut lines. Blacks growing up in a society dominated by white culture became unavoidably influenced by a "color consciousness" that resulted in color prejudice within the black community. Some darker-skinned blacks accused mulattoes of putting a "premium on a fair complexion." Although victimized by prejudice like other blacks, some mulattoes did attract criticism by displaying a form of cultural elitism. In Nashville, Cleveland, and Washington, D.C., mulattoes formed controversial "Blue Vein" societies, excluding all but blacks whose skin was not light enough to see blue blood coursing through their veins. Even some churches appeared to cater only to lighter-skinned individuals.[4]

Most mulattoes thought of themselves as members of the African American community and sought to dissociate from exclusionary groups. Those whose birth and education gave them an advantage over most darker African Americans identified intellectually and emotionally with the hardships faced by blacks. The major role assumed by the mulatto elite revolved around the idea of racial uplift. For most, education, economic development, and protection of political rights took center stage. Through his labor, educational, and political activism, Wright Cuney exemplified the post-Reconstruction mulatto elite. At the time of his death in 1897, blacks continued to advocate such goals, but Jim Crow laws led to a divergence of views among the next generation on how best to proceed. According to historian Kevin Gaines, "Amidst legal and extralegal repression, many black elites sought status, moral authority, and recognition of their humanity by distinguishing themselves, as bourgeois agents of civilization, from the presumably undeveloped black majority;

hence the phrase, so purposeful and earnest, yet so often of ambiguous significance, 'uplifting the race.'"[5]

Two leaders in the early twentieth century, Booker T. Washington and W. E. B. Du Bois, became synonymous with racial uplift, though with differing ideologies and concepts. The two men's backgrounds could not have been more different. Washington, born a slave in 1856, graduated from Hampton College in Virginia and in 1881 founded Tuskegee Institute in Alabama. He favored an accommodation with whites. According to Washington, "the wisest among my race understand that the agitation of questions of social equality is the extremist folly." He opposed a liberal education for the mass of African Americans and publicly opposed members of the black elite who promoted such an education. Washington argued that most blacks could advance best if they pursued a trade through industrial education. Furthermore, blacks could gain the respect of whites, not through politics, but through the accumulation of wealth. Political agitation in Washington's view was counterproductive, for blacks first had to prove their worth through property ownership and community self-help.[6]

Du Bois, born in 1868 in Great Barrington, Massachusetts, studied at Fisk University, the University of Berlin, and became the first black Ph.D. from Harvard. His criticism of the accommodationist approach had a substantial effect on the eventual diminishment of Washington's ideas in the eyes of most African Americans. A prolific author, Du Bois and others, formed the NAACP in 1909. Du Bois edited the NAACP's official publication *The Crisis: A Record of the Darker Races* for over twenty years. His ideas and outlook changed over time, but through his early books such as *The Philadelphia Negro* and *The Souls of Black Folk* and his essay "The Talented Tenth," Du Bois dominated black intellectual thought in the first half of the twentieth century. Next to her father, no other person had a greater influence on Maud Cuney-Hare than her close friend Du Bois.[7]

In striking out on a new course of racial uplift, Du Bois openly criticized Washington. In *The Souls of Black Folk,* Du Bois wrote that "the prevailing public opinion of the land has been too willing to deliver the solution of a worrisome problem into his hands, and say, 'If this is all you and your race asks, take it.'" Privately, Du Bois told friends that Washington stood "for Negro submission and slavery." He further criticized Washington for establishing a "false distinction" between industrial and liberal arts education that created a chasm between black elites and the masses. Du Bois argued instead for the creation of a "talented tenth" comprising college-educated African Americans who would provide the leadership necessary for uplifting the race. In a precursor to the tactics of Martin Luther King Jr., Du Bois advocated black agitation and protest, leading to what most African American leaders until that time did not advocate: social equality. He had complete faith in the ability of the educated black elite to effectuate this change.[8]

Du Bois's more radical course fit well into ideas of uplift long advocated by many within the northern black elite. Instead of the materialistic approach of Washington, they were committed to social uplift based upon "Christian ideas of sacrifice and service" arising out of the antislavery movement. Within this realm, black women in the late nineteenth and early twentieth centuries played an important role. While attending college in Boston, both Maud Cuney and W. E. B. Du Bois became part of a close circle of friends who assembled at the Charles Street home of Josephine St. Pierre Ruffin. There, they came into close contact with Boston's freeborn black elite that included William Monroe Trotter, Angela and Francis Grimke, and Geraldine Pindell. The wealthy widow of a municipal court judge and a "militant suffragette," Ruffin strongly influenced the black women's club movement. Du Bois called Ruffin's home a place "where college-bred African Americans met and ate, danced and argued and planned a new world." Later, Cuney-Hare actively participated in the League of Women for Community Service, founded by Ruffin.[9]

In his *Autobiography*, written seventy years after he first met Maud Cuney, Du Bois fondly remembered that "she was a tall imperious brunette, with gold-bronze skin, brilliant eyes and coils of black hair; daughter of the Collector of Customs at Galveston, Texas. She came to study music and was a skilled performer. When the New England of Music tried to 'jim crow' her in the dormitory, we students rushed to her defense and we won. I fell deeply in love with her, and we were engaged." The two never married, but their friendship remained close until her death in 1936.[10]

Among black male leaders of the early twentieth century, only Du Bois appeared to advocate a strong role for black women. His feminist views derived from his strong-willed mother and later by his association with Josephine Ruffin. Most other black male leaders ignored the role of African American women. Irrespective of such attitudes, African American women contributed their own ideas of racial uplift. Cuney-Hare's parents, childhood, education, and personal interests had a direct influence on her vision and future course.[11]

Born February 16, 1874, Maud Cuney had a privileged childhood when compared to most black children of the late nineteenth century. Through her parents, her musical interests developed at an early age. Wright Cuney, who learned to play the violin from another slave, "Henry the fiddler," at his father's home in Houston, often performed publicly. He later developed a love of Irish ballads and Italian operas and passed that appreciation on to Maud. Besides her "beautiful" soprano voice, her mother, Adelina Cuney, played the piano. By the time of her high school graduation, Maud Cuney too had become an accomplished pianist. She often accompanied her father on trips to the eastern seaboard, where they attended various plays and cultural events. As she came of age, Maud Cuney received a cultural education that few black or even white children could hope for. Thus, in a childhood filled with literature (including Shakespeare), music, and other cultural endeavors, she seemed destined for a life in the arts.[12]

With a personal wealth variously estimated at between $50,000 and $150,000, Wright and Adelina Cuney could provide the best possible education for their children. Maud Cuney's dreams of a career in music and the arts had little chance of being fulfilled in the South, where most black liberal arts colleges with limited budgets could not provide a musical education. Other African American institutions specialized in vocational training. After Maud graduated from Central High in Galveston, her parents sent her to spend the summer in Newport, Rhode Island, while they decided which northern institution she should attend. They chose the New England Conservatory of Music and enrolled her for the fall of 1891. Founded in 1867 in Boston, Massachusetts, the conservatory was then (and remains to this day) the oldest independent school of music in the United States. Modeled after similar European institutions, and at the time dominated by a European faculty, the conservatory provided students with an education in liberal arts and classical music.[13]

Besides being the most prestigious college of its kind, skin color did not appear a concern for the conservatory's administrators. Boston, after all, had a rich abolitionist history, while Massachusetts leaders Charles Sumner, Henry Cabot Lodge, and Wright Cuney's old friend Windell Phillips had led the battle for black civil rights in the U.S. Congress. The black Republican leader had made many trips to Boston over the years, and most likely the school faculty knew who he was. Maud's parents probably foresaw no problems for her in Boston. Another African American, Florida L. Des Verney, daughter of a wealthy mulatto cotton dealer in Savannah, Georgia, also enrolled in the conservatory. Both resided in the same dormitory, but when white southern students learned the two young women were living on campus, they immediately asked for their removal.[14]

Cuney did not know of an earlier incident in 1884 involving a black female student. Then, few southern whites attended, and when they asked for the black students removal the administration refused. Since 1884 the reputation of the school had attracted white southerners in larger numbers, and according to the *Boston Courant,* southerners now outnumbered their northern counterparts. Fearing a loss of tuition, the administration wrote to Cuney and Des Verney requesting that they find their daughters homes off campus. "We have a large number of pupils who are affected by race prejudices, and the Home must be conducted so as to insure the comfort and satisfaction of the largest number possible, otherwise its success, and the success of the Institution, which is entirely dependent upon its patronage, is imperiled."[15]

The conservatory strongly implied that they could not guarantee the women's safety if they remained. Even before Maud Cuney consulted with her father about what to do, she told the school's administration that she would refuse removal. In a strongly worded letter, Wright Cuney refused the school's request and criticized the administration for dishonoring the "noble men and women" of Massachusetts, who in the past fought against prejudice. He pointed out that their "publications and catalogues" stressed principles "fixed in the foundations of humanity, justice and honor. And not subject to the control of a few misguided girls and parents." Cuney went on to say: "You request my co-operation in surrendering to the demands of prejudice, by withdrawing my daughter; I cannot help you. Ask Massachusetts; ask her mighty dead; ask her living sons and daughters. They will co-operate with you, if you cannot solve the problem, and render your Institution illustrious throughout all ages."[16]

The conservatory's actions quickly became an issue within Boston's black community. By the 1890s, attitudes among many whites toward African Americans in Boston began to change. In 1889 Henry Grady of the *Atlanta Constitution* and propagandist for the New South, made a well-received and well-publicized speech in Boston extolling the virtues of the supposed new industrial South. He spoke of the progress the "kindly and dependent race of Negroes" was making in this system. At the same time, a split developed between Henry Cabot Lodge and other Boston Brahmins over the necessity of Lodge's proposed federal election bill pending before Congress. Incidents of discrimination against blacks in restaurants and other public places began to take place. A general decline of support among many within the white community toward black rights characterized Boston into the early twentieth century. Nevertheless, Boston was not Atlanta. Although small in number, the black elite continued to maintain a position of some prominence.[17]

Wright Cuney's old friend T. Thomas Fortune, editor of the *New York Age,* and other well-known African Americans outside Boston also spoke out against the conservatory's actions. Some blacks called for the legislature to revoke the school's charter. Du Bois and other black students from Cambridge joined in the protest. Then the Colored National League, a New England civil rights organization, called a special meeting to deal with the issue. The members condemned the school's actions as "an unwarranted and gross insult" to Boston blacks. They made no demands for social equality, for to do so, "we would feel obliged to associate with many whites from whom we would naturally turn with repugnance," but resolved "Conservatory of Music do nothing or permit nothing to be done that will disgrace Massachusetts and tend to give credit to the oftrepeated assertion that she is no further advanced in the right direction than is South Carolina or Georgia."[18]

Under such intense pressure, the conservatory reversed itself and agreed to allow the young women to remain on campus. Des Verney nevertheless arranged for his daughter to live elsewhere, but Cuney stoically remained. "I refused to leave the dormitory," she wrote, "and because of this, was subjected to many petty indignities. I insisted upon proper treatment." Cuney's talent earned the respect of her instructors, who treated her well. Her father praised Maud for standing up to school administrators, telling her: "You were quite right, darling, when you said that you knew your father would tell you to stay. I can safely trust my good name in your hands. I wish you were where I could embrace and kiss you." Boston blacks continued to be upset with the conservatory and the lack of support from Boston whites. In Cambridge that year, African Americans made the school's actions a campaign issue, providing the votes necessary for the defeat of Richard Dana, a school trustee, in his race for mayor.[19]

Cuney continued her pianoforte studies at the conservatory. For a time, she earned extra money by playing the piano professionally while attending classes. Overall, she had a rich experience in Boston. She continued to see Du Bois and took part in the active social life of the city's black elite. In 1892 Cuney accompanied Du Bois, Monroe Trotter, and others to Amherst for the graduation from the University of Massachusetts of two black men, William H. Lewis and George Forbes; both were classmates of Calvin Coolidge. According to Du Bois, while there, an issue of the *Crimson* mention both him and "his Maud." Later that year Du Bois received a scholarship from the Slater Fund for study in Europe.[20]

When Du Bois left for Europe, he also left Maud. Neither Cuney nor Du Bois mentioned what became of their engagement. Both may have decided that it could not continue when they would be so far apart. More likely, Du Bois decided to end the engagement because of his developing attitude toward marrying a woman of lighter complexion. Throughout his adult life, Du Bois viewed a dark skin color as a matter of racial pride and later wrote, "As a sheer matter of taste, I wanted the color of my group to be visible." Du Bois later married a woman "whose physical characteristics were as racially ambiguous" as Cuney's. Although the engagement ended, through the years, their friendship only strengthened.[21]

Upon graduating from the conservatory, Cuney continued her education at Harvard's Lowell Institute, studying English Literature, a subject dear to her father's heart. Her music studies continued too. Her parents engaged two of the leading piano teachers on the East Coast, both Europeans residing in the United States, to continue her music instruction. One, Edwin Klahre had studied under Franz Liszt, the famous composer and father-in-law of Richard Wagner. The other, Emil Ludwig, had studied under famed pianist Anton Rubinstein and formerly taught at the St. Petersburg Conservatory for Royal Ladies, which Rubinstein helped create. Cuney also studied music theory under Martin Roeder, a leading music theorist.[22]

With her father's health deteriorating and his political fortunes diminishing by then, Cuney moved back to Texas to be close to him. She accepted a position as music director of the Deaf, Dumb, and Blind Institute for Blacks outside Austin. Wright Cuney had been instrumental in the school's creation. He often visited his daughter and his son, Lloyd, who attended Tillotson College. Cuney's pianoforte instructor Emil Ludwig also made frequent trips to Texas for her continued studies.

Lloyd Garrison Cuney

Shortly before Wright Cuney's death in 1897, Ludwig planned a concert for Maud Cuney at the Austin Opera House. As in the past, she came up against racism. The opera house did not refuse Cuney a concert, but the management refused to seat blacks and whites together. African Americans who wanted to see a black performer would have to sit in the balcony. The two canceled the appearance and moved the concert to the institute. Wright Cuney attended with many of his friends, including T. Thomas Fortune from New York. After the death of his wife and his repudiation as Texas Republican leader, Maud's concert was a source of great pride to him. The Austin papers lavished high praise upon her performance.[23]

As the "adoring daughter of an adoring father," a very close and loving relationship had existed between the two. When Wright Cuney passed away, his death left a great void in her life. She seemed embittered and disillusioned over his treatment by his former supporters and the Republican Party. This may account for why she never became politically active, even though she later became friends with other African American women active in the suffrage movement. Cuney continued teaching at the institute. While in Austin she met J. Frank McKinley, a mulatto physician over twenty years her senior; the two married in late 1898. As one of only a few black physicians in the state, McKinley had a large number of black patients, but the immense poverty of most black Texans made it impossible for him to obtain the wealth and prestige he apparently wanted. He convinced Maud to move to Chicago. Thus began a tragic period in her life.[24]

McKinley convinced Maud to disavow her black heritage and pass into the white community as "Spanish Americans." Their Caucasian features and light complexion made this a viable option, at least physically. "Passing" became very controversial among whites, who often delighted in exposing those found out. Although controversial among blacks, many understood that "passing was the only means of gaining an equal opportunity." For those who successfully entered the white world, the passage came with heavy social and emotional costs. Not only did they have to abandon friends and relatives but also endure the constant threat of possible exposure.[25]

From the beginning, Maud felt uneasy with the change. Although two of her own aunts and one cousin had passed into the white community, her actions contradicted everything her father had taught her. He proudly identified himself as "Negro" and tried to instill that pride in his children. In her biography of Wright Cuney published in 1913, she recalled an incident that took place while the two attended the Republican National Convention in 1892. One morning the attractive eighteen year old preceded her father to breakfast. According to Maud, "the cashier noticed my sitting alone, and coming to the table she began the conversation by asking if I was waiting for my husband." When Cuney explained she was waiting for her father, the cashier responded, "Oh, Spanish girls marry when so very young, we in the hotel thought that you were a little Spanish girl bride." When Maud told her she was a "Negro," the woman refused to believe it: "but you and your father must be Spanish! No? Then Creole—surely you cannot be colored." Wright Cuney praised Maud for "declaring" her race. She wrote, "He abhorred above all things the supposedly easier way of 'passing for white,' and instilled in my young brother and me a hatred and contempt for the cowardly method which is upheld by many who can successfully disown their Negro blood."[26]

The displeasure she knew her father would have felt about his daughter passing for white added to her unease in an increasingly unhappy marriage. For a time, Maud tried to make the most of living in Chicago. While her husband's practice flourished, and while keeping her true identity a secret, she became active in racial uplift through Chicago's settlement house movement. Jane Addams's Hull House, founded in 1889, set the example others would follow. Maud became one of many young educated women using their talents to fulfill the humanitarian needs of the slums. Nowhere was this need more evident than in the black ghetto of Chicago. Even before the "Great Migration" of African Americans in the 1920s, large numbers of southern blacks had come to Chicago. Massive unemployment and the status of unskilled workers plagued many of the city's blacks. Maud worked in the settlement house of the African Methodist Episcopal church, giving piano lessons and performing at socials. Through her work in the black community, Maud may have come into contact with a small but growing number of educated southern blacks "who were not content to live life on Southern terms." Chicago also had a significant number of African American women's clubs involved in racial uplift. The racial pride exhibited by other educated African Americans and black women's groups may have influenced Maud's decision to return to her roots.[27]

Cuney's settlement work, although satisfying, did not make for a happy marriage. Her efforts with other African Americans while hiding her own identity must have weighed heavily upon her conscience. In 1900 the couple had a daughter, whom they named Vera and, at the insistence of McKinley, identified her race as Spanish American on the birth certificate. Within a year of Vera's birth, Maud could deny her identity no longer and returned with her daughter to Texas. She joined the faculty of Prairie View Agricultural and Mechanical College as a music instructor. In 1902 McKinley filed for divorce.[28]

In the combative proceedings that followed, McKinley could no longer keep his identity a secret. Although he received a divorce in Maud's absence, she returned to Chicago for a contentious custody battle over their daughter. The case became a sensation in the black press. Her lawyer attacked the credibility of McKinley by exposing his false pretensions of being a Spanish American. In the process McKinley expressed what the *Chicago Broad Ax* called his "disgust with Negroes." His lawyer charged Maud with leaving her husband without cause and implied the possible endangerment of their child. In an era when the mother's overall custodial rights were far from guaranteed, the judge gave McKinley custody of Vera. When Maud remarried in 1906, she refiled for a change in the custodial agreement, which afterward allowed her to keep Vera for the three summer months each year. Tragically, Vera died in 1908.[29]

Maud's passionate love affair with music and the arts had little chance of fulfillment in Texas. She loved the state and even arranged for burial alongside her parents when she died, but the opportunities for a black professional woman outside teaching did not exist. Her brother had also graduated from college and moved to Washington, D.C., becoming a civil service clerk and an official in the Congregationalist church. In early 1904 Maud moved back to Boston to pursue a career in music. On August 10, 1904, she married William Parker Hare, a member of "an old and well-known Boston family." She pursued a life rich in music, theater, and writing there.[30]

Only in the late twentieth century have the contributions of African American women of the late nineteenth and early twentieth centuries begun to receive recognition from historians. As the rest of her life shows, Cuney-Hare deserves a prominent place in that history. Her experiences with racism at the New England Conservatory of Music and in Texas as well as her upbringing as the daughter of an influential southern black politician who dealt with black issues on a daily basis establish Cuney-Hare as a woman in touch with the hardships faced by other African Americans. Her privileged position compared to other blacks and level of education mark Cuney-Hare as a member of a small and influential black elite.

Unlike some within the African American elite who maintained a certain "aloofness from the masses," Cuney-Hare strove to engage them. Even
in her short experience of "passing" as someone not of black heritage, she
participated in uplift activities in Chicago's black ghetto. Eventually, she
found it impossible to turn her back on her own blackness and proudly
proclaimed her identity. Her friendship with W. E. B. Du Bois and her
education placed her among the highest circle of the African American
intelligentsia of the early twentieth century. Thus, Maud Cuney-Hare
rejected the accommodationist approach and endeavored to improve the
lives of other African Americans through music and the arts.

CHAPTER 7

Maud Cuney-Hare

Musician, Director, Writer

WRITING TO W. E. B. Du Bois in June, 1928, Maud Cuney-Hare stated: "The days and nights have been crowded—the Allied Arts Centre continues to grow. The Players produced *Antar of Araby* on May 15. The success was flattering! A full house—not only colored spectators— but an appreciative audience drawn from Boston's most cultured circles. My experiment in the Allied Arts is winning sympathy and our play receipts will provide our studio maintenance until late fall." Cuney-Hare had made a success of her life in Boston. Besides managing the Allied Arts Centre that she created, producing and directing plays, writing articles on African American music, and collecting material for her book on Negro musicians, Cuney-Hare had a full schedule of concerts and lectures across the eastern seaboard. She told Du Bois: "I have my own vision, and I'm free to try my wings. Of course, they may get broken, but we do not look forward to any serious falls." She had inherited her father's optimism and work ethic. As a woman and as an African American, she met the challenges and succeeded in the face of immense odds.[1]

Cuney-Hare's parentage, upbringing, education, and financial status placed her within the "upper class" of early-twentieth-century African Americans. While black elites had developed characteristics that differentiated them from the mass of other blacks, white society tended to view them as part of that mass. Gunnar Myrdal, in his landmark study *An American Dilemma: The Negro Problem and Modern Democracy*, appropriately identified white views in terms of a "caste" system in which all African Americans, regardless of complexion, education, or wealth, "are subject to certain disabilities solely because they are Negroes." White views and racial perceptions also affected and complicated class relations among blacks. According to historian Adelaide M. Cromwell, "The perception that the upper class is different from the masses, yet inseparable from them, has created a state of mutual ambivalence within the Negro class structure making it difficult for one class to lead or for others to follow."[2]

For their part, the elite rejected both white views and black ambivalence. The mulatto elite, perhaps naively, believed their mixed heritage gave them a special status that allowed them to act as intermediaries between whites and blacks. They sought to use their status to become deeply involved in issues affecting African Americans. Obtaining equality for all black Americans became an overriding goal. To achieve this, many within the elite sought to uplift the mass of African Americans through education and cultural enlightenment and hoped this would "soften" white prejudice. Eventually, they believed the majority of blacks would reach such a point that whites would accord all African Americans civil rights and equality based upon "individual merit and achievement." That goal appeared similar to the view of Booker T. Washington, but the elite often used different methods based upon a more diverse ideology. Through her uplift work in music and the arts, Maud Cuney-Hare epitomized many of these views.[3]

African Americans in Boston made up a much smaller percentage of the population than in many other large northern cities. In 1890, Boston had a black population of 8,125, constituting only 1.8 percent of the population. Twenty years later the number of blacks had increased but still made up only 1.9 percent of the total population. Within the black community, 62 percent were of southern birth in 1910. Five in six African Americans in Boston faced either unemployment or immense poverty. Black Bostonians lived in integrated neighborhoods alongside immigrants from eastern Europe and Russian Jews. Blacks attended integrated schools, where they made up only 10 percent of the student body.[4]

Increasingly during the early twentieth century, the powerful white Brahmin elite, who previously had strongly supported black civil rights, backed away from that goal. At the same time, the Irish majority took over city politics. Few Irish politicians, except one-time mayor John

"Honey Fitz" Fitzgerald, appeared sympathetic to African American rights and concerns. Along with black migration from southern states, the new influx of immigrants from Russia and eastern Europe also caused tension. Both Brahmins and Irish politicians, who rarely agreed, resisted these new immigrants. Attitudes toward eastern European immigrants, who most Anglo-Americans considered inferior to western Europeans, had residual effects on white attitudes toward African Americans. As the twentieth century progressed, heightened racial friction characterized white and black relations in Boston.[5]

The black elite knew that the racial cooperation that had characterized Boston more than any other city during much of the nineteenth century had ended. Although economic differences between upper-class African Americans and the mass of black Bostonians continued to widen, white prejudice tended to bring the two groups closer together. Though small in number, the leadership exerted by the elite went well beyond Boston's city limits. Besides the involvement of Josephine Ruffin in the black women's club movement, Monroe Trotter and his newspaper, the *Guardian,* had a large black readership outside Boston. As the son of James Trotter, a former Union officer in the black 55th Massachusetts Regiment and the first black Democratic recorder of deeds in Washington, D.C., Monroe Trotter became one of the more radical of black leaders. He virulently opposed Booker T. Washington and his ideas and through his newspaper led a sometimes vicious campaign to discredit the accommodationist. Washington countered with an equally ferocious attack on Trotter and others who opposed him. Many of the intellectual arguments both for and against accommodation derived from the city's black elite.[6]

Cuney-Hare's move to Boston again brought her into close contact with Du Bois, who moved to New York City in 1909. It also coincided with a new and exciting development for individuals dedicated to black equality and opposed to the dominating influence of Washington. In 1905 Trotter and Du Bois called together a group of noted black Americans. Meeting at Fort Erie on the Canadian side of Niagara Falls, they organized what became known as the Niagara Movement to protest segregation and infringements on black civil rights. Despite opposition from Trotter, the group allowed female participation in 1907, and Cuney-Hare became one of the first women to join. While the movement had little success, it led directly to an alliance with a number of whites sympathetic to the cause that included Oswald Garrison Villard. This alliance led to the founding of the National Association for the Advancement of Colored People. In 1910 Du Bois became editor of the NAACP's magazine, *The Crisis: A Record of the Darker Races.*[7]

The Crisis reflected the "militant journalism" of Du Bois. He attacked American racism head on, sought to tell the truth about lynching, and exposed antiblack governmental policies. Through his editorials, Du Bois sought to radicalize black opinion by attacking the white establishment. He also wanted the magazine to reflect the accomplishments of African Americans, their literature, art, and music. He convinced many of the best and the brightest in the black community to contribute, usually without remuneration, to the magazine's success. Before her writing and concert schedule limited her time, Cuney-Hare edited the music section of the magazine. Afterward, she contributed articles on and about black music. The magazine also reported on her exhibits and concerts, and her activities became a fixture in its monthly issues. Cuney-Hare's biography of her father, published in 1913, remained on *The Crisis's* recommended reading list for the next ten years.[8]

Shortly after her second marriage and her move to Boston, Cuney-Hare became involved in black-upper-class cultural activities, affiliating her with that society. Scholars studying Boston's black upper-class have identified it as composing only 2 percent of the already small black population. The upper class in the early twentieth century consisted of "lawyers, physicians, salaried employees, business proprietors, literary and musical people, and the like, who are distinguished by superior education and refinement." They usually owned their own homes and sometimes, as in Cuney-Hare's case, owned summer homes along Boston's shoreline. Their professions often brought them into close contact with the white community, and for many their livelihood depended as much on white patrons as black. In most cases, though not always, they were of light complexion. Several black elites, especially families of free-born backgrounds, had a reputation for exclusivity "that went beyond that of those in Washington or Philadelphia." Cuney-Hare, though a member of the upper class, strove to be inclusive. Through her activities in the arts, she sought to include people of all races and classes.[9]

Cuney-Hare already had many friends and contacts in Boston, formed while attending the Conservatory of Music, but her marriage to William Parker Hare helped solidify her position in Boston's black upper class.

Rarely did this upper crust allow southern African Americans to become part of their society, but Cuney-Hare's family background, education, light complexion, and marriage gained her quick acceptance. Although little is known about William Hare, he seems to have been a member of a well-established black Boston family. While not listed in the city directories of that period, during the Great Depression he received what Du Bois called a "sizable pension" that aided the Hares through the hard times faced by most Americans.[10]

Boston in the early twentieth century had many social and cultural organizations, but only two appeared limited exclusively to the black upper class. Shortly after moving to Boston, Cuney-Hare became a member of the executive committee of one of these organizations, the St. Mark's Musical and Literary Union. Founded in 1902, the union pursued the "moral and intellectual improvement of the community" and exemplified many of the goals sought by the black elite who pursued racial uplift. Its meetings, held Sunday afternoons at St. Mark's Congregational Church, attracted large audiences of black and white attendees who listened to performances, lectures, and addresses from well-known black and white Bostonians. According to one observer, "More noteworthy than prepared talks is the extemporaneous speaking from the floor, in which the Negroes exhibit a mental grasp and ability in debate calculated to surprise uninformed white visitors."[11]

Although not a member, Cuney-Hare on several occasions lectured on black literature and black music before the other upper-class organization, the Boston Literary and Historical Association. While similar to St. Mark's, the association, founded in 1901 by Archibald Grimke and Monroe Trotter, held meetings outside predominately black districts, stressed a more politicized agenda, and became a forum for "militant race opinion." Both groups challenged Washington's accommodationist approach. They also became outlets for elite social gatherings that included galas and fundraising events and acted as organizational liaisons with black students at Harvard and other area institutions. Because of their financial position and the status of the membership, both associations believed themselves to be the cultural leaders of the extended African American community.[12]

Cuney-Hare began to establish personal and artistic relationships with leading African American literary and musical figures both inside and outside Boston. Like her, these educated and talented young people represented a new generation of African Americans born after Reconstruction. Cuney-Hare, who inherited a love of poetry from her father and may have written some herself, began to collect poems written about trees after moving to Boston. Eventually, she compiled this collection into an anthology published in 1918 entitled *The Message of Trees*. Dedicated to her daughter, Vera, who died ten years earlier, and bound in an expensive wooden veneer binding, the book contains over 170 poems by various poets and short essays written by famed environmentalist John Muir. While only one poet, Paul Lawrence Dunbar, appears to be African American, the book represents a significant achievement.[13]

William Stanley Braithwaite, a young black Bostonian, poet, and literary critic, wrote the book's introduction. The two friends would collaborate on other projects as well. Born December 6, 1878, Braithwaite published his first collection of poetry, *Lyrics of Life and Love*, in 1904. Cuney-Hare and Braithwaite had similar outlooks toward their art and race. He wrote that art spoke "the universal language of human nature; and if I ever carry any distinction to the grave, it will be in proving that art, and especially art as it has developed and been perfected under the influence of American civilization, with all its peculiar paradoxes, knows no distinction of race." Similarly, Cuney-Hare wrote: "Many Negroes as well as Anglo-Americans admit that the so-called American Negro is no longer an African Negro. Apart from the fusion of blood he has for centuries been moved by the same stimuli which have affected all citizens of the United States. They argue rightly that he is a product of a vital American civilization with all its daring, its progress, its ruthlessness, and unlovely speed. As an integral part of the nation, the Negro is influenced by like social environment and governed by the same political institutions; thus we may expect the ultimate result of his musical endeavors to be an art-music which embodies national characteristics exercised by his soul's expression."[14]

Though Cuney-Hare had diverse artistic interests, music took center stage in her life. Following her move to Boston, she began almost immediately to perform publicly. She formed friendships and musical relationships with other young black musical talents who had a direct effect on the development of African American music in the first half of the twentieth century. One friend, Clarence Cameron White, often collaborated with Cuney-Hare, even composing music for her four-act drama *Antar of Araby*. Born in Tennessee in 1879 to a mulatto physician, White

studied violin at the Oberlin Conservatory of Music and in Europe before moving to Boston. Many music critics considered White to be the
"foremost black violinist" of the early twentieth century, and he later
performed at the White House for Franklin and Eleanor Roosevelt.
Cuney-Hare found special significance in White's use of black rhythm
and folk themes in many of his compositions.[15]

Cuney-Hare formed her closest and most productive musical partnership with William Howard Richardson. He was born in Liverpool, Nova
Scotia, in 1869 to a Canadian family of English, Dutch, and African descent
that moved to Cambridge, Massachusetts, in 1880. Recognized at an early
age as a gifted singer, Richardson received vocal training from several of
the leading East Coast vocal coaches. A baritone soloist for several white
churches in the Boston area, including St. Peter's Catholic Church in
Cambridge, Richardson performed as the only black singer in the Boston
Philharmonic Society. He also sang in the Roland Hayes Trio; Hayes
became the first African American male to win worldwide acclaim as a
concert performer. By 1910, Richardson had become one of the leading
black baritones on the East Coast. After a concert by Cuney-Hare and
Richardson in 1919, Olin Downes, the music critic for *The New York Times*
wrote: "Mr. Richardson, who was born with a beautiful voice, gave proof
of his unremitting industry, his artistic purpose, his consistent growth.
He is not merely a maker of musical sounds. He gives these sounds
dramatic significance. He sings not merely a melody but a poem, and
rightly fits the tone, in its color and inflection, to the text. The quality of
his voice remains fundamentally rich and full."[16]

The two performed together for over twenty years. Their partnership
and exploration into black music had an influential effect on the growing
interest among African Americans in their own culture. Cuney-Hare
made many trips to the Gulf Coast, Puerto Rico, Cuba, Haiti, Mexico,
and other areas researching the roots of African American music. She
collected African American music wherever she went, much of which
would have been forever lost to future scholars without her preservation
efforts. Based on her research, Cuney-Hare developed a lecture and concert series with Richardson. Her series became so popular that her two
booking agencies, the Eastern-Empire Lyceum Bureau and Biggs and
Company, had to arrange concerts a year or more in advance.[17]

Cuney-Hare also formed an impressive exhibit of African musical
instruments and music, black historical photographs, and other black

musical memorabilia. Presented in museums and libraries along both the
East and West Coasts, it received great interest from whites and blacks.
One particular item became a source of pride for African Americans and
a great surprise to many whites. Cuney-Hare presented previously un-
seen copies of letters between Ludwig van Beethoven and George
Augustus Bridgetower. Bridgetower, the son of an African who immigrated to Europe and a white Polish woman, gained widespread recognition as a violin prodigy. Referred to in musical circles as the "Abyssinian
Prince," the former student of Haydn became a close friend of Beethoven.
The famous composer wrote the *Kreutzer Sonata* specifically for the black
virtuoso. Although he lived in Europe, the introduction of Bridgetower
to the black community added to the cultural awakening of black Americans in the 1920s that became known as the Harlem Renaissance. The
exhibit became a source of great pride for the NAACP, which used it
whenever possible. *The Crisis* reported of one such exhibition: "In
Wanamaker's great store on the second floor a beautiful room was filled
with things that illustrated the rise and development of Negro music.
There were African musical instruments, pictures of Negro artists and
composers, musical scores and programs, books and articles—so many
so carefully gathered matters that picture the mighty work of the black
man in music. Hundreds of people entered daily, asked questions and
lingered. It was an education for white Philadelphia and the teacher and
founder was Maud Cuney-Hare of Boston."[18]

Cuney-Hare's concert series, articles, and book sought to enlighten
and create pride among blacks for their musical heritage. She also sought
to create an appreciation among African Americans for European classical music. Cuney-Hare knew firsthand that music schools and other
educational institutions controlled by whites did not recognize the
contributions of African Americans to the country's musical heritage.
Often, white musicians and others who came into contact with black
music failed to credit the black performer and composer as the source of
their own works; many just stole the music and put their own name to it,
a practice well documented as late as the Rock-and-Roll era of the 1950s.
By the early twentieth century, much of black music had either blended
with white music or become an undifferentiated part of American culture.
The black institutions that offered music courses may have wanted to
explore black musical contributions, but they had little material and few
financial resources to draw upon. Cuney-Hare and others like her knew

that in a racially prejudiced society, African Americans had to save their own musical heritage.

Her concerts and recitals received support from elite black patrons along with a few enlightened whites. Usually, the concerts took place in sold-out auditoriums, churches, and concert halls across the Northeast and as far south as Virginia. The program sometimes began with classical songs or piano pieces by Scarlatti, Handel, Chopin, Beethoven, or Massenet. Performances before the Samuel Coleridge-Taylor Society or other elite black organizations sometimes comprised only classical renditions.[19]

These associations exemplified the desire of many black elites to separate themselves from the "minstrel caricatures of blackness" popular with many whites. According to historian Kevin Gaines, "Eurocentric images and ideals of respectability were central to elite blacks' aesthetic tastes." The Samuel Coleridge-Taylor Society, named after a British composer of African descent who transcribed and orchestrated "Negro spirituals with West African folk melodies for the concert stage," represented a way for African American elites to improve musical tastes while showing black music in a positive manner.[20]

While she agreed with many of the goals of such organizations, Cuney-Hare's own philosophy reflected a more diverse approach. She deplored the "comedy and buffoonery" of the popular minstrel shows but respected the talent of those black performers involved in such acts and the sophistication of many of the musical scores. She found that hidden in some minstrel performances and behind the "offensive racial terms and scenes" were subtle expressions of defiance against the dominant white culture that black audiences could appreciate while whites remained blinded by racial stereotypes. Some black performers who got their start in minstrel shows moved on to lift "Negro music above the plane of the so-called Coon Songs" and compose and perform musical comedies and dramatic productions for black audiences.[21]

Cuney-Hare did not want to limit herself to a small and select audience. She saw music as a vehicle to enhance the broader African American community and directed much of her attention to them. Most of her concerts comprised "Afro-American" folk songs, African American spirituals, Louisiana and Spanish Creole folk song renditions, and music from South and East Africa and the West Indies. Arranged by Cuney-Hare, much if not most of the music had a significant relation to African American musical roots. Frequently, as in a concert presented at the Columbus Avenue A.M.E. Zion Church in Boston in 1912, the program presented only black composers.[22]

Often, Cuney-Hare and Richardson presented "costume" recitals. Before the Brooklyn Academy of Music, the pair performed in elaborate costumes and received excellent reviews. According to one critic: "Mrs. Hare and Mr. Richardson received one of the heartiest receptions seen in years. The Academy was literally jammed to capacity." Cuney-Hare wrote to Du Bois: "I'm sorry that you did not hear the recital. I believe you would have enjoyed the program. At any rate, the audience did so. Standing room was taken and encores demanded." Cuney-Hare and Richardson often received critical acclaim, usually in white newspapers, which had the resources to employ music critics. Philip Hale, music critic for the *Boston Herald,* praised one concert as "excellent" and "dramatic," leaving the audience "wanting to hear more Afro-American music and Creole Folk Songs." *Musical America* reported: "The accompaniments to most of the songs were arranged by Mrs. Hare, who is making a special study of our southern music and thereby doing a valuable work in bringing to light these folksongs, which have so far been neglected, but which are well worth knowing for enjoyment as well as for the appreciation of their importance in our national musical development."[23]

Cuney-Hare received high praise for her "music talks." Her lectures included information on African American music and its roots as well as "Creole Folk Music" gleaned from research collected during her extensive travels. In her lectures she repeatedly stressed an enduring theme in her life, the artistic training of young people. Wrote one critic: "Mrs. Hare talked in an instructive and interesting manner, about the origin and character of music. She is a fluent speaker, fortunate in her choice of words. Nor is she too didactic in giving information." In a concert at Rochester, New York, the *Democrat and Chronicle* reported: "Maud Cuney Hare offered to music-sated Rochester quite a new sensation in the old Creole and black folk songs for which she herself has arranged the music and made the translation. In her informal talks about folk music she was particularly charming, and she was at her very best in the interesting group of songs and dances of the Creoles."[24]

As Cuney-Hare traveled the Northeast performing and lecturing, Du Bois watched her career with great interest. Throughout their correspondence, Cuney-Hare and Du Bois discussed their personal lives, successes, frustrations, and work. Du Bois offered her not only his support, encouragement, and help but also provided helpful criticisms when he thought it necessary. Cuney-Hare did not shy away from criticizing Du Bois, but overall a deep-seated respect existed between the two. Whenever Du Bois came to Boston or Cuney-Hare went to New York, the two tried to meet, if only for a short time. While both remained very fond of the other, no evidence points to anything but a very close friendship. Cuney-Hare felt a special pride in Du Bois's career and took very seriously his goals for African Americans and her participation in the movement. Writing to Du Bois in 1924, Cuney-Hare stated: "Your achievements have given me particular pleasure, for I know full well that you richly deserve all the honors that have come to you and more. You have never swerved from your devotion to a Cause to which you dedicated your life some years ago. To those of us who were apart of those early days, belongs the joy in the recognition that you have fulfilled the promise of a consecrated life. You can afford to ignore those who have chosen to see your acts through darkened glasses."[25]

The Harlem Renaissance of the 1920s began an exciting and busy period for Cuney-Hare and other writers and African Americans musicians. At first the revival became apparent in black literature. The writings of James Weldon Johnson, Claude McKay, William Braithwaite, Langston Hughes, Du Bois, and many others are credited with beginning the era. Then African American musicians began to turn their attention to black folk music. According to historian Eileen Southern, "they exploited the rhythms of Negro dances and the harmonies and melodies of blues, spirituals, and the newer music called jazz in their concert music." While this trend seemed new to many of the new black intelligentsia, Cuney-Hare already had spent sixteen years researching, writing about, and performing such music. Her influence on the flowering of the renaissance can be measured in several ways. Besides writings in *The Crisis* and in other publications, her performances, literary collaboration with William Stanley Braithwaite, and musical collaboration with Clarence Cameron White, Harry T. Burleigh, and other composers and musicians made Cuney-Hare an important participant in the cultural movement.[26]

At the beginning of the decade, the *New Music Review* announced the publication of Cuney-Hare's collection of Creole folksongs, stating: "One awaits eagerly the book of Creole songs that Mrs. Cuney-Hare is editing. Mrs. Hare, by birth and early environment, is well qualified to edit and annotate these songs." Cuney-Hare came into contact with Creole music as a young woman in Galveston. She became fascinated by the mysterious and beautiful songs sung by the black laborers from New Orleans her father brought to the Galveston docks during white labor strikes. A Creole neighbor living in Galveston identified the songs as Louisiana Creole music. As a young woman, she began to collect and research this musical style. Cuney-Hare described Creoles as a distinct people and the "descendants of the original French or Spanish settlers and the women of the land of whatever blood, white or colored." As a child of mixed racial heritage herself, having a white grandfather, she identified with the ambivalent nature of creolism.[27]

Cuney-Hare researched the origins of several different groups of people of color and their relation to folksongs, both Creole and African American. She traced some Creole folksong roots to "Negroes" from Santa Domingo who migrated by way of Cuba to New Orleans during the war between Napoleon and Spain in 1809. Cuney-Hare also credited the influence of Latin American Creoles of "Iberian, Indian, and African blood" to the Louisiana musical style. She severely criticized whites who referred to Creoles with some black heritage as "Negro Creole." "To call their music Negro Creole," she wrote, "is absolutely incorrect and shows a woeful ignorance of the history of that particular section—a distortion of the facts that even rising prejudice does not excuse." She also rejected attempts by the Louisiana legislature to deny some their heritage by defining many Creoles as white, while others who previously had been considered Creole in the eyes of the law became mulattoes and octoroons. Cuney-Hare wrote: "In 1908, Louisiana, with the unbridled increase of racial hatred and prejudice, under 'Act 87,' gave the Creole element of so-called 'white admixture only' a classification with the whites, thus at the same time distinctly classifying the mulatto and octoroon, [but] as the Supreme Court of the State of Louisiana correctly states that a person of mixed blood is not a Negro. But even the passing of laws cannot obliterate history woven in song."[28]

Cuney-Hare found very little written about Creole music or people and came to her own conclusions based on the origins of their music: Creole music "of the New World was brought over from Africa to South American countries and to West Indies, thence to Louisiana and its bordering territories, shaped by French and Spanish influences, after which it became a distinctive folk-song inheritance of America." Cuney-Hare

Maud Cuney-Hare

found that Creole folksongs were "wed to the dance." "The dances are no longer generally practiced, but the folk-songs remain. They bear the same characteristic rhythms as the more familiar Aframerican melodies and odd scale progressions and structural form of Latin folk-Song. A number exhibit Spanish influences. The themes are but few and those are of the primal emotions. There are far more love songs than are to be found in any other section of the South. The work songs and those of wood and water are easily traceable to Negro influences and customs. The usual manner of traveling by boat brought forth many boat songs, and as in West Africa, the rowers are particularly fond of singing in the moonlight as they rowed to their song."[29]

In the summer and fall of 1921, Cuney-Hare and Richardson toured the West Coast and received "a good reception and good reviews." She published four different articles in 1921, including "Africa in Song" in *Musical Observer* and one for *The Crisis* entitled "Ethiopian Art." The ancient African kingdom, ruled by African kings for a millennium, held special significance for black Americans in search of racial pride and their historical roots. *The Crisis* took a special interest in Haile Selassie when he became emperor of Ethiopia in 1916 and followed his reign for the next fifty-eight years. Black Americans, especially intellectuals, hoped the discovery of their African roots might help create racial solidarity.[30]

Cuney-Hare took a special interest in the sixth-century Arab-Abyssinian poet-warrior Antarah ibn Shaddad al-'Absi and seventh-century African mulatto musician Mabed Ibn Ouhab. In what may be a metaphor for racial uplift, both figures "won their freedom because of their marked superiority and extraordinary gifts." Cuney-Hare wrote articles on both for *The Crisis*. Antarah became the subject of her play *Antar of Araby*. With resonate symbolism for the 1920s, the story of Antarah takes place while he is in slavery. It begins when his father, a tribal leader, captures his mother, who is a "beautiful" slave. His father rationalizes his love for a black woman, stating: "In Blackness there is some virtue, if you observe its beauty well. Were it not for the black mole on a fair cheek, how would lovers feel the value of its brilliancy? Were not musk black it would not be precious. Were it not for the black of the eyes where would be its beauty? And thus it is that black ambergris has the purer fragrance!" While slaves and slaveowners loved and admired Antarah's poetry and his ability in battle was unequaled, his blackness and slave status denied him his freedom and the woman of his affections. The play ends with Antarah gaining both, though only after gaining the respect of enemies and friends through his extraordinary deeds on the battlefield.[31]

By 1924, Cuney-Hare had finished an early draft of her book on black musicians. Shortly afterward, she received a plea from Carl Engel, music librarian for the Library of Congress, to try to publish it quickly. At that time the library had almost no information on African American music. Engel complained that the only thing he had to send to the many requests concerning the subject was a list of "colored musicians" given him by Cuney-Hare. Unfortunately, Cuney-Hare could find no publisher who would take her book. Frustrated, she wrote to Du Bois: "The manuscript of my History of Afro-American music is still at the house—two or three publishers have spoken well of it, but think it too expensive a proposition, in that the book would appeal to a limited class of readers. I am tempted to break it up in parts, but it ought to be published as it is. It is needed." Her friend advised to prepare abstracts for publication in *The Crisis* and through her other contacts as a way of presenting her work to the public but held out no hope that this would be successful. Cuney-Hare would have to wait another twelve years before a publisher agreed to take her book. During that time, she and Engel developed a close working relationship that proved beneficial to both.[32]

Undeterred by the lack of a publisher, Cuney-Hare continued to add information and revisions to the manuscript. She also continued to turn out articles, present concerts, and show her exhibit. Wellesley College asked her to exhibit the collection at its library and give a series of lectures on black music. "Isn't that rather nice," she wrote to Du Bois. She continued a heavy work schedule. In January, 1925, Cuney-Hare wrote Du Bois of her "many irons in the fire." Besides having concerts booked solid for the next two years, the *Christian Science Monitor* wanted to publish two more articles and wanted her to do a series of book reviews. About her concerts, Cuney-Hare told Du Bois, "You will be pleased at the growth of singer and pianist—it has been such a high climb!" He also wanted an article for *The Crisis* and wanted her to send information on black music to his contacts in the Soviet Union.[33]

In addition to her heavy schedule, she had the burden of caring for her ill mother-in-law, who became an invalid under her care. Shortly afterward, an exhausted Cuney-Hare also fell ill. Although not fully recovered, she soon went back to work, but for the rest of her life, illness plagued her. She seemed to feel her poor health a personal weakness, writing to Du Bois, "isn't it too bad that music with me is but a mirage! I am not proud of my frailty." Her spirits received a lift in the fall, when students from her Musical Arts Center performed her play *Antar of Araby* for a small group of friends and neighbors. Shortly after moving to Boston, Cuney-Hare began to give piano lessons out of her home, which she formed into a small center for "teaching piano and theory and offering lecture courses in music history and appreciation, studio musicales, exhibits, class lessons, and library research services." The success of her

venture led her to think in terms of creating a larger arts center that
would include a theater group and would carry her ideas on racial uplift
to all African Americans in Boston.[34]

Cuney-Hare began 1926 by taking a trip to Guadeloupe, Cuba, and
Puerto Rico. Du Bois had planned to see her before she left but at the
last minute could not travel, writing: "I was so very sorry not to get down
to see you off. Bring me any photographs that you can get hold of and
write me any interesting data." He promised to write about the trip in
The Crisis. Cuney-Hare returned refreshed and ready to act upon her
idea of a little theater. She learned that Du Bois planned to come to
Cambridge to speak at Harvard and wrote to tell him of her plans.

> I am hoping to have an opportunity to talk with you about a
> project which is close to my heart. I want to establish a music cen-
> tre that will eventually develop into a Community Art Centre. The
> "Antar" production last winter was a venture that proved my faith
> in the capabilities of a group of boys and girls who are eager to do
> other things.
>
> I want a Music school that will embrace an experimental
> children's Little Theater. I am trying to find my way—meanwhile
> there are a number of young graduates here who are eager for me to
> find an opening.
>
> I have followed—somewhat—Russia's experiments in music and
> the drama. I wish you might have time to tell us something of what
> is being done in that country. I have not a penny to start my ven-
> ture, but I am making plans just the same. I have all the friends
> needed from Boston's music world—who are most sympathetic.[35]

To many African Americans mired in poverty, or even the black elite
who felt oppressed by their own government, the idea of a political system empowering the powerless had a great appeal. Du Bois took his first
trip to the Soviet Union in 1926 and returned sympathetic to what he
perceived the Communists were trying to do. In his autobiography,
Du Bois wrote: "The Soviet Union is trying to make the working man
the object of industry. His well being and his income are deliberately set
as the chief ends of organized industry, directed by the state." In the arts
the Soviets rejected the old Czarist approach and sought to enlighten the
unenlightened by creating a new experimental approach. With virtually

no American examples to follow, Cuney-Hare at least wanted to know what new approach the Russians were pursuing.[36]

Funding for the arts center became the first major obstacle Cuney-Hare would have to overcome to make her dream a reality. Not until Franklin Roosevelt's Works Progress Administration, and later the Kennedy and Johnson administrations of the 1960s, did the U.S. government begin to fund the arts, so Cuney-Hare would have to find other sources. She first tried to find a philanthropist to support her venture but failed. Undeterred, she went on to establish her center. Shortly before she began on her new venture, she had succeeded in convincing the South End Music School, which catered only to whites, to open its doors to African Americans. She then became the only black member of the board. Impressed by Cuney-Hare's success in opening up the music school, the black League of Women for Community Service offered to help. The league found a location for her proposed Allied Arts Centre. To Du Bois she wrote: "I am doing this under the Leagues' name—not independently—and while under my sole direction I want it known as the Art Centre of the League of Women for Community Service. Forwarded by colored women, it cannot be called a segregated movement. Meanwhile there is opportunity to meet the cultural needs of the young folk."[37]

The location, in downtown Boston across from the New England Conservatory of Music and a block from Symphony Hall, could not have been better placed. Cuney-Hare wanted the center open to all races. She already had a number of white students studying piano at her music school and hoped the new organization would attract both blacks and whites. She wrote about that idea to her good friend and African feminist Adelaide Casely Hayford: "If I am fortunate in securing this place, it will mean that I can put our young folk's talent and wares in a section that will be in the regular stream irrespective of race. I abhor the segregated districts." In an interview in the *New York Age,* Cuney-Hare expanded further on her ideas: "The Allied Arts Centre plans to work along the lines of the new art movement in America. Our interest in the Little Theater is not expressed in an edifice of endeavor and creative work. Through our art classes we aim to cultivate friendliness with all racial groups. Two Japanese boys are registered in a Saturday class. We are opposed, you see, to the idea of separateness, and hope, through conscientious work, to become one of the noteworthy streams in making of an ideal New England and American spirit."[38]

While inclusive of all races, Cuney-Hare's emphasis in the Allied Arts Centre offered an outlet for talented young black playwrights and aspiring actors and actresses. She financed the center using her own funds, with receipts earned from its productions, and with a small number of donations. As managing director she refused a salary or income from the venture and established an advisory board comprising several leading citizens in the black community and others involved in the arts of Boston. Beside being a little theater, the center advertised a long list of activities, including eurhythmics, practice drama groups, music-study clubs, group and carol clubs, art classes, and children's theatrical work shops. The center's motto, "To Bring Art to the child, through the child to the home, from the home to the Community," clearly reflected Cuney-Hare's own vision of racial uplift.[39]

She and Richardson presented concerts at the center on a regular basis. To officially open the new center, she presented a Beethoven-Bridgetower evening for her friends and supporters. Not everything went smoothly with the facility, as Cuney-Hare noted in a letter to Du Bois: "I have been working very hard to properly establish our art centre, more so because no end of jealousy and envy have sprung up. I have been greatly surprised." Jealousy aside, Cuney-Hare had inherited many of her father's political skills and put them to good use, attracting both public interest and patron donations.[40]

Tragically, as happened so often in Cuney-Hare's life, bad news followed good. In January, 1928, she received news that Joseph Cuney, her uncle and her father's last surviving brother, had died in Galveston. Ill at the time and under a doctor's care, Cuney-Hare was devastated when she wrote to Du Bois: "My darling Uncle Joe lies dead in Galveston and I can't go to him. The world is a very lonely place to me right now. Could you use his picture in the Crisis? He was a man of distinction—a successful lawyer with more white than colored clients—a book worm—a fine scholar. A man of local prominence as he always held fine positions. Like my father, he idolized me." Although in poor health and grief stricken, Cuney-Hare quickly returned to work by directing three plays in three months and writing two articles. After the productions she proudly told Du Bois that not only did the plays attract a full house but also "the audience included quite a number of distinguished white friends who came to see just what the Allied Arts players were capable of doing. They declared that the artistry of the performance was a revelation to them." After a play presented in April, she wrote Du Bois, "Professor Belford Forrest of Emerson College declared that our workshop play was worthy of being produced by any theatrical organization."[41]

By 1928, probably because of the success of Allied Arts, Cuney-Hare began to reduce the number concerts she performed. She continued to perform five to eight concerts per year, and her relationship with Richardson remained close. Richardson had created his own vocal school, which also became a success. Cuney-Hare remained a prolific writer of articles. In October of that year, the *Musical Quarterly* published her twenty-page history, "Portuguese Folk-Songs." She continued to produce and direct plays, mostly by African American playwrights, including several by Georgia Douglas Johnson. Born September 10, 1886, in Georgia and a graduate of Oberlin Conservatory of Music, Johnson may be best known for her poetry. She published *The Heart of a Woman* in 1919 and *Bronze: A Book of Verse*, a series of poems dealing with racial issues, in 1920. Like most of Cuney-Hare's female friends, Johnson was a feminist. With special resonance for Cuney-Hare, Johnson's poetry and other writings often examine the difficulties faced by black women who against great odds wanted to pursue a professional life. Johnson wrote one poem specifically about Cuney-Hare, entitled "To Your Eyes."[42]

With the onset of the Great Depression in 1929, hard times began to descend on much of the country. The Allied Arts Centre continued to presents plays and carry on its other activities, but economic conditions may have begun to take a toll. Cuney-Hare wrote to Du Bois, "I am at the Arts Centre day and night, holding on to it, altho it is still carried by faith-there is no money." Hard times may not have been as hard for her personally. In 1930 she went on an extensive trip to Central America. While in Costa Rica, she marveled at the blending of races, writing to Du Bois, "The lines of racial color blend so completely in that section that it is difficult to distinguish the particular shade of brown or yellow at which the colored Costa Rican turns white!" Throughout her travels and writings, Cuney-Hare strove to understand why race had such a negative determination in American culture but so much less on others.[43]

In March, 1930, she asked Du Bois to serve on the board of the Allied Arts Centre. "He would be glad to as long as there are no meetings to attend," Du Bois replied. By 1930, his reputation among blacks appeared at its peak and his name alone would add status to the center. But for the first time, in May, 1930, the center engendered some controversy. Cuney-

Hare produced and directed William E. Easton's play *Dessalines*. Wright Cuney had written an epilogue for the play when it was published in 1893 entitled "A Tribute to Haitien Heroism." Cuney described Dessalines, who served under Toussaint L'Overture, as possessing "the ferocity of the Nubian lion, the undaunted heroism of the Spartan, and an unquenchable hatred of the whites." That hatred, Cuney noted, had been born of the bloody excesses of the French. The initial performance took place before a packed house on May 15, 1930, but the subject matter appeared too controversial for Boston's newspapers. Cuney-Hare wrote to Du Bois: "for the first time the leading newspapers were silent with no reviews. The Negro papers gave mention of the play only when paid. I had no idea that a play of Haiti in the Napoleonic period written 30 years ago would be taboo."[44]

In the summer of 1930, Cuney-Hare decided to buy a second home at Squantum, then an exclusive suburb just outside Boston along the shore. She wanted a secluded place where she could rest from her hectic schedule and the beach seemed perfect. The exclusive area apparently had no black residents. Again, Cuney-Hare would come up against New England racism but characteristically refused to yield. She wrote to Du Bois:

It really looks now as if I shall have a home at Squantum by the fall, so I will get some rest in September. The house would have been up by August first had not the color question been rampant. I submitted a bid on my first lot, and then the fun—I partly owned three other lots within three weeks time. "Murder" was out before the last papers were signed, but just as fast as one cut up on my hands, I tried another. I made up my mind that was the section I wanted to live in and how laughable the whole matter was. Each succeeding lot was better than the first and this one is prettiest of them all, and right in the midst of pretty cottages—all year round house owners. So! When they wake up, they will wish they had allowed me to land in the first place where there was a few vacant lots to separate us. I have rights too to the private bathing beach.[45]

Soon after Cuney-Hare closed the deal on her new house, she received bad news. Lloyd, her brother who lived in Washington D.C., had contacted tuberculosis. Bedridden with the disease in both lungs, he remained in his sister's care until his condition forced her to arrange for his

confinement in a private clinic at Asheville, North Carolina. After seeing both parents ravaged by the disease, she sadly knew the ultimate
outcome of Lloyd's illness. Her spirits received a lift in early 1931 when
Cuney-Hare found a publisher for her book on black music. The offer
came from black historian Carter G. Woodson. After earning a Ph.D.
from Harvard, Woodson began the *Journal of Negro History* in 1916. In
1921 he began the Associated Publishing Company with the expressed
purpose of publishing books, articles, and photographs of and by African
Americans. Woodson wanted some changes in the manuscript such as
adding information on Creole music that Cuney-Hare had not included.
Pleased to have finally found a publisher, she wrote Du Bois: "Life is so
queer. I have worked so long and faithful in this field with never any
financial backing to make leisure undisturbed. Is there yet a chance for
me to hew my own way out."[46]

Woodson considered Cuney-Hare's *Negro Musicians and Their Music,*
the "crowning achievement" of an "amazing career." In his review of the
book, Woodson wrote that Cuney-Hare "was interested not only in the
music that Negroes have produced, but in the musicians themselves. At
the same time she presented in this volume more of the philosophy un-
derlying this contribution of the race than can be found in any other
volume extant." Cuney-Hare ventured into unchartered waters when she
commenced on her massive study. She sought to examine the entire history of black music from its African roots to the jazz age. Only one book
on black music preceded hers, James Monroe Trotter's *Music and Some
Highly Musical People* (1878). His book, according to Eileen Southern, was
"invaluable for the unique information it provides about black musicians
of the nineteenth century, both as individual artists and as members of
groups." An amateur musician, Trotter acted as an agent for several black
musicians and personally knew many of those he wrote about. A general
study, *Music in America* by Louis Frederick Ritter, published in 1883, takes
little notice of African American contributions. While others in that field
wrote articles about black music, only *Negro Musicians and Their Music*
presented a comprehensive scholarly approach.[47]

In fifteen chapters Cuney-Hare explored African roots and influences,
black folksongs and themes, and African American musical pioneers as
well as musicians of her own time. Her study of African music relied upon
an impressive collection of sources, from British explorer Sir Richard Burton
to leading late-nineteenth-century scholars Leo Frobenius and A. B. Ellis.

Although the attitudes of many of those researched by Cuney-Hare reflected the racial prejudice of the period in which they wrote, she did not feel limited. About Burton, Cuney-Hare wrote, "His work would have been more valuable, however, had he not so often descended to flippancy and ridicule." Therefore, she cautiously used their observations to arrive at her own conclusions. As a trained musician, she could compare African rhythm, melody, and idiom with that of black American music to find similarities.[48]

Cuney-Hare's analysis of black folk songs found peculiarities that did not appear in any other American or European music but could be found in African songs. She stated, "among a number of Negro folk songs, we find that in the majority of them the cadences progress downward and that phrase before the first accent of a measure just as is done in true African song." The "rhythmical relationship and melodic similarity" between the two continents illustrated a "strong root of African ancestry." While she acknowledged the "universality of certain principles of design" found in all folk music, she also identified characteristics found only in "native African music and that of the Negro folk song." Cuney-Hare argued that just as the Irish, Scots, and Italians exhibit certain characteristics derived from their musical heritage so too did African Americans. She wrote, "the ingenuity shown in the shifting of accent or addition of grace notes and embellishments to give contrast in different repetitions; in the manner of reiteration of the same figure or phrase at higher levels; and, in the enhancement of tonal coloring given by intricate rhythmical clapping of hands and patting of feet—these qualities produce a folk musical contribution that is unique and apart."[49]

Upon arrival in America, slaves recreated many of the musical instruments used in their homeland. Cuney-Hare's personal collection included many of these devices made from trees, reeds, and bone. When used in African American song and dance, they produced the same "rhythmic patterns" as among many African peoples. In an analysis of religious and sentimental songs, Cuney-Hare found similarities with African songs, especially in their demonstrative emotional nature and the use of metaphor, and a direct relation between African American metaphors and African folklore. She wrote, "its freedom and lack of restraint mark it apart from that of the pallid and repressed music of the so-called Nordic races."[50]

Even though slaves were forced to give up their native tongues and learn English, their music often reflected the meaning and dialect similar to the many languages of their homelands. According to Cuney-Hare, "It is not surprising that those Africans brought as captives to America found it difficult to express themselves in the words of a newly-heard language and that the meaning of the words in a number of the oldest songs should be obscure." In the "Negro dialect" of America, "all harsh letters such as G, D, T, and R, are softened or eliminated, while as in Latin-America, the V is blurred to B." Therefore, Cuney-Hare found that when Anglos changed the dialect and words of a "Negro Spiritual" for their own use, they also detrimentally changed its meaning. The hymns and "shouts" of African Americans, she argued, often reflected the satire or "taunts" generally found in African songs but never found in Anglicized hymns. Cuney-Hare researched approximately eight hundred spirituals and plantation songs to reach her conclusions. One example she used came from an old spiritual from Alabama, "Redeem, Redeem":

> Some go to church an' dey put on pretense
> Until de day ob grace is spent.
> Ef dey haven' been changed you'll know it well,
> When Gabriel blow', dey will go to hell.
> Sunday come' dey'll have Christian faith,
> Monday come' dey will lose deir grace;
> De Devil gets in dey will roll up der sleeve
> Religion come out an' begin to leave.[51]

In a chapter laden with emotion, Cuney-Hare took on the white musical establishment. White musical scholars of the late 1920s and 1930s led an eVort to preserve, catalogue, and discover the origins of American folk and spiritual music. In so doing they ignored black musical origins, thus black music in their eyes became white. John Powell, a leading white music authority, argued "that the Negro heard the songs credited to him as they were sung by Anglo-Saxons, and being inherently musical, he took them and made them his own." Another authority, George Pullen Jackson, argued that the black spiritual "was the product of the Methodist camp meeting revival movement." Many of the same scholars believed that most black folksongs had English origins. Cuney-Hare, as did many other African Americans, found these claims ridiculous. She wondered about the state black music would be in had their spirituals actually come from Methodist revivals or their folk music from the "barren" English folk songs and caustically dismissed such claims: "Since the revival movement did not begin to develop in the United States before the last quarter of the 18th century, it is difficult to believe that a race whose forbears were as musical as the Negro, should remain musically inarticulate for over 350 years—until they heard the wan, inane camp-meeting tunes which it is claimed, they sang as their own."[52]

Before the Civil War, whites had the advantage of publishing their own songs and those stolen or adapted from slaves, but as Cuney-Hare bluntly stated, "the publication of Negro spirituals in hymnals does not make them white." White scholars claimed that because spirituals had Hebrew influences they could not have derived from illiterate slaves. Cuney-Hare responded to such logic by pointing out the obvious to scholars who should have known better, that in any society without the written word, oral tradition takes its place. She dismissed such prejudice-biased assumptions by pointing out the importance Moses had to an enslaved people and that "Apart from the fact that the Biblical text of the Old Testament was assimilated by the slave in his acceptance of the Christian religion, there is a sympathetic affiliation which is not surprising."[53]

Cuney-Hare's many travels and research made her an authority on the folk music of Cuba, Puerto Rico, and the Virgin Islands, and in her study she expanded in detail upon its influence and relationship to African American music. "[T]heir special contributions will help us to understand those made by the Negroes along the Atlantic and Gulf Coast." The "Afro-Cuban" native music, a mixture of African primitive music with early Spanish influences, could be found among the "Creoles and Negroes of Louisiana." Dance-song melodies like the "Bamboula" could be found among blacks all along the Gulf Coast. She wrote about black roustabouts who, up and down the Mississippi, danced to the same music found throughout the West Indies called Counjaille, or Counjai.[54]

A recurring theme throughout *Negro Musicians* stressed by Cuney-Hare was "music as art." She divided her concept into two sections: "Folk Music—that of the illiterate, the unsophisticated; of the unknown bard, welding a communal experience into a complete whole, whether it be that of sorrow or joy; and Art Music—the output of trained musicians whose creative works, composed according to an accepted standard of beauty, give aesthetic enjoyment to the cultured." As a classically trained musician, she had studied folk influences in the music of Europe. Cuney-Hare, like many other African Americans, viewed with pride Dvorak's use of "Negro melodies" in his *New World Symphony*. She supported the idea of using black folk themes in "art music" and discussed in depth the African American composers who were pursuing that goal, believing, or at least hoping, that this movement would become the future course of black music. She had developed friendships with many of these composers. Her close friend Henry F. Gilbert of Cambridge had written several symphonic works based on "Negro themes." Gilbert's *Comedy Overture on Negro Themes* received widespread attention throughout Europe and among the black upper class.[55]

Cuney-Hare had definite opinions about her hopes for the future of African American music and took a dim view of the spread of ragtime and jazz. "So far did the Rag craze and Jazz spread," she wrote, "that in traveling and visiting many institutions of learning, the author found that the musical taste of the youth were being poisoned." She believed that the new musical forms were destroying "an appreciation of the classics" and prevented an "acquirement of taste for good poetry." Cuney-Hare applauded efforts by some "high-minded school presidents" to preclude students who were only interested in ragtime or jazz from using musical instruments. She has a more favorable view of the early "blues" movement as developed by W. C. Handy, which she believed represented a "type of folk secular music," but disliked the overt sexuality of the blues music that came out of the 1920s.[56]

Her criticism of jazz reflected her musical education and her own bias of what "good music" should be. "Jazz," Cuney-Hare argued, "will divide itself and follow two strains—The Negro and the Intellectual." She identified "two classes of native composers." Composers like Clarence Cameron White and Henry T. Burleigh represent the intellectual, whose "created works are those which are apprehended by the intellect and emotions." These composers, she wrote, "are of the school of rising young composers of Negro descent who are creating music as an art. Their work follows the line of Negro music as it has grown from the African or Negro folk song, expressive of the soul of a people in their varied moods, but the material is treated as by men of education, musical training and creative intelligence."[57]

She believed composers of jazz reduced music to the "physical and sensational" and ran counter to ideals of racial uplift. As a southern black woman only one generation removed from slavery, Cuney-Hare may have felt the sensual nature of the "new music" would only reinforce white

racial prejudice about black morality. Yet her criticism of the music did
not extend to the talent of the many jazz performers and composers like
Cab Calloway, Don Redmon, Eubie Blake, and Duke Ellington. Cuney-
Hare admired their ability, originality, and use of "Negro idiom and
rhythm." She hoped that "thoughtful musicians" then experimenting with
jazz rhythms and color might eventually elevate the medium. She believed that they would come to realize "that no seeker after beauty can
find inspiration in the common combination of unlovely tones and sug-
gestive lyrics. Music should sound, not screech; Music should cry, not
howl; Music should weep, not bawl; music should implore, not whine."[58]

Cuney-Hare thoroughly researched dozens of African American "musical pioneers" dating from the late eighteenth century. Most resided in
large northern cities or in New Orleans, a city with a large free-black
population. She discovered singers like Thomas J. Bowers, a brilliant
Philadelphia tenor born in 1836, who received high praise from white
newspapers. He chose to sing opera "to show to the world that colored
men and women could sing classical music as well as the members of the
other race by whom they had been so terribly vilified." Black female
singers like Elizabeth Taylor-Greenfield, living in Buffalo, New York, in
the 1840s and 1850s, performed to audiences of both races and gained
fame in Europe. Besides vocalists, Cuney-Hare catalogued numerous
violinists, cellist, and piano virtuosos. Many African Americans of talent,
she noted, could not gain acceptance in America but did find success in
Europe. One of many examples, Edmund Dede was born a free black in
New Orleans in 1829. An accomplished violinist and conductor, he immigrated to France and became director of the L'Alcazar Orchestra in
Bordeaux.[59]

The uplifting quality of music and her views on black musical progress
reflected those ideals. During her lifetime, Cuney-Hare had witnessed a
tremendous growth in black musical appreciation, especially since 1900.
By 1930, the United States had "10,583 colored musicians and teachers."
While white institutions discounted black contributions, by the 1930s
African American colleges and schools routinely turned out black musicians and instructors. She added to this growth through her own music
and theater activities. Even new musical forms like jazz, which she found
objectionable, owed much to this expansion. Cuney-Hare, of course,
looked with greatest pride on the development of music that reflected
her own interests. Most major cities had black music societies, whether

they were choral groups like the Fisk Jubilee Singers or music societies like the Samuel Coleridge-Taylor Society. Clarence Cameron White, Harry T. Burleigh, and many other African American composers had become successful in the black community and gained recognition by many whites. Several black musical groups and individual performers gained recognition through appearances before Presidents Herbert Hoover and Franklin Roosevelt. African American music, she believed, would become "an integral part of the nation." Cuney-Hare also received recognition herself. In 1931 the New England Federation of Churches passed a resolution praising her work in Boston, and the next year the American Missionary Association recognized her for her contributions to racial uplift.[60]

Cuney-Hare appreciated receiving the recognition but continued with her work. In early 1932 she began writing a series of articles about black folksongs of the Virgin Islands, a project that reflected her many visits to that part of the world. As her writing progressed and the Allied Arts Centre continued to thrive, however, her health began to deteriorate. In April, when pain racked her upper left side, her doctors scheduled her for exploratory surgery. The results proved to be inconclusive, but this event began a long process of declining health. She wrote to Du Bois that "altho in daily pain, I have some manuscripts before me that I work at a bit every day." Doctors assured her that she could eventually return to her beloved piano. Shortly after she returned to her home in Squantum to rest, her husband, Will, became ill and confined to bed as "an invalid for some time to come." Stoically, Cuney-Hare accepted the additional burden and by May had completed the first article on the Virgin Island folksongs.[61]

Cuney-Hare spent the rest of 1932 trying to recover. Caring for Will put her work for the center on hold. After reading an article denigrating the contributions of African Americans to American spirituals in the *Mercury*, she discovered the same writer planned to publish a book of "White Spirituals." She wrote Du Bois that the writer had "taken over bodily our Negro songs. It irritates me to say the least and I do so want to answer him!" Her illness precluded her from responding, and she ended the year back in the hospital. This time doctors discovered a tumor on her left side they previously had missed. In Chicago on a speaking tour, Du Bois did his best to encourage her: "No one knows better than I how difficult a siege you have had but perhaps after all this will be the turning point. I remember in my own case that my hospital experience helped me be more careful and consequently healthier than before. I hope that when you are feeling better and have the strength you will write me a word."[62]

While surgeons operated and successfully removed the cancerous tumor, Cuney-Hare suffered severe nerve damage. Still, doctors held out hope that she would eventually recover the use of her arm. Confined to bed for the next three months and in constant pain, she began the final revisions on her book and continued to write Du Bois with ideas for the future, offering him encouragement. She suggested having a "Music-Study Club" for young people in *The Crisis*. "I have a small children's music club in Squantum all are white. There is so much that could be given to colored children if only it could be brought to them. Everything is sorely changed but there is still the future before us with its possibilities." She remained optimistic that she could return to the piano and offered to do a benefit lecture and recital tour for the magazine the following year. Cuney-Hare worked hard to complete her manuscript revisions while debilitating pain kept her from her music.[63]

In 1934 Du Bois wrote that *The Crisis* could not start any new ventures like a music study club because of a financial crisis faced by the NAACP. The depression had left many its members unable to pay dues. Du Bois also informed her of his increasing difficulties with the association's directors over the direction of the NAACP. He felt the problem "is such that the organization must be entirely re-organized or I shall leave it definitely." In August Du Bois resigned from the organization he had helped create twenty-eight years earlier.

Cuney-Hare's health never recovered and gradually grew worse over the next eighteen months. In one of her last letters to Du Bois, she apologized for not writing more, telling him: "I am in such trying irritating pain—never a day free from it since I was operated on. I miss my music, that is the ability to play for myself, and can't but get discouraged when acute pain keeps me from playing." She concluded by telling him, "I do hope you are going to have the freedom to do just what you would rather do, and let's hope it will be for your-self." Maud Cuney-Hare died two days before her sixty-second birthday on February 14, 1936.[64]

On the seventeenth memorial services took place at St. Peter's Episcopal Church in Cambridge and at the E. L. Morrison Chapel in Boston. Conducting the services were students of the Allied Arts Centre, including a group of young actors, a string trio who played some of Cuney-Hare's favorite music, and readings by former Allied Art players. Floral arrangements came from dozens of friends and organizations all over New England, including composers, music societies, literary figures, and performers. Burial took place at Lakeview Cemetery in Galveston next to her parents. Two months later Carter Woodson published *Negro Musicians and Their Music.*[65]

In a long editorial written several months after Cuney-Hare's death, Du Bois summed up her life: "Her inflexible refusal to compromise with cheapness and prejudice were the target of sneers, envy and good will. She knew deprivation, insult and lack of understanding; yet she seldom flinched; she seldom faltered; she walked the continuing goddess through life, despising the Color Line; communing with the masters, teaching and believing the best; always planning good and fine enterprises, writing books and articles and traveling. . . . She was in her extremity of need and ecstasy of pain so magnificently self-sufficient, alert, determined, unafraid, always refusing to be hemmed in and conditioned by the provincialism of race."

As Du Bois so poignantly wrote, Cuney-Hare rejected the limitations placed on blacks by white society. The fact that she had advantages most African Americans did not have played only a minor role in her success. If advantages alone determined a person's achievement in life, then an untold number of white men and women with the same advantages would have been as successful, but they were not. Cuney-Hare may have defined the difference herself in a letter she wrote Du Bois about her plans for an Allied Arts Centre: "I have my own vision, and I'm free to try my wings."[66]

Through the study and research of black music, Cuney-Hare understood that African Americans had not only a cultural heritage of which they could be proud but also one kept from them by a society dominated by prejudice. She then undertook to present that purloined legacy to the black community. In addition Cuney-Hare acted upon her ideas of racial uplift. Her concerts and lectures brought African American music directly to people of both races. Through the Allied Arts Centre, she provided a forum for black playwrights, actors and actresses, and artists. The fact that she attracted students and audiences of different racial backgrounds underscored her commitment against the "color line." Cuney-Hare's "crowning achievement," *Negro Musicians and Their Music,* placed her firmly as a member of the Black Renaissance and provided an invaluable history of African American music.

Like so many fine books written by African Americans in the early twentieth century, *Negro Musicians and Their Music* did not receive the recognition it deserved. Besides a racial bias held by many whites against African American authors, the Great Depression reduced the number of people who could afford new books. Except for the *Christian Science Monitor, Musical Observer* (for which Cuney-Hare had contributed articles), and the *Journal of Negro History* edited by Carter Woodson, few periodicals reviewed her book. Her death two months before publication reduced its publicity, for the book lost its most important spokesperson.

For those fortunate individuals who came into contact with *Negro Musicians and Their Music,* the book had a significant power. Although very young when Cuney-Hare died, Josephine Harreld Love, who wrote the introduction to the 1996 reprint of that volume, knew the book well. Love's father, Kemper Harreld, owned an original copy. She wrote, "I do not recall a time during earlier years of my life when the name Maud Cuney-Hare was not referred to, although I have no memory of having seen or met her in person." Love went on to become a pianist, musical scholar, and director of Your Heritage House, an art museum for young people in Detroit, Michigan, that she established in 1969. Cuney-Hare no doubt influenced many others like Josephine Love.

In many respects, the life of Maud Cuney-Hare defies categorization. As a member of the African American elite who pursued racial uplift, she opposed the development of ragtime and jazz because she believed such forms harmed the artistic, literary, and musical advancement of young blacks. She favored the pursuit of proper musical training that the improvisational nature of jazz did not provide. Cuney-Hare often promoted western classical-music appreciation as a way of racial uplift. In so doing she reflected the dominant views of others in the black elite identified by Kevin Gaines, but Cuney-Hare in many respects transcended that limited view. She appeared just as comfortable with African American folk music, work songs, and spirituals as she did with Mozart. Cuney-Hare saw the preservation and promotion of black musical heritage not only as a way of racial uplift but also as a way to cultivate racial pride through the development of an African American cultural identity. Her Allied Arts Centre, lectures, concerts, and writings reflected a much broader view than those held by most members of the black elite.

CHAPTER 8

Conclusion

PHILIP CUNEY did not live to see his mulatto son rise to leadership of the Texas Republican Party or become an important civic leader, a labor organizer, and the collector of customs at Galveston. Nor did he see his granddaughter become a concert pianist, musicologist, and important member of the northern black elite. Would Philip Cuney have recognized his African American descendants or at least have taken pride in their accomplishments? In many ways Philip Cuney seemed a contradiction. As an antebellum planter he believed in the institution of slavery and sought to maintain that system. He exploited his powerful position as a slaveholder to begin a sexual liaison with his house servant Adeline Stuart. Yet by freeing his slave family and providing them with an education, Philip Cuney recognized on a basic level the humanity of Adeline and their children. In these respects Philip Cuney epitomized Joel Williamson's slaveholding maverick.

The influence Philip Cuney had on his son Norris Wright Cuney appears significant. Wright Cuney, like his father, went into politics. Although a Republican, his political philosophy echoed the limited view of government espoused by Philip. Like his father, Wright Cuney provided an education for his own children. While he never acknowledged publicly his relationship to Philip, Wright Cuney seems not to have criticized him privately. Maud Cuney-Hare suggested this in her biography about her father when she wrote in respectful and positive terms regarding her white grandfather. She gave no indication of any mistreatment by Philip of his slave family or of any hostility harbored by Adeline and her children toward him. Often, former slaves did not openly criticize their former masters because of fear of retribution by the owners or their families. Yet as a man of some power and influence who had little to fear from such reprisals, Wright did not do so. Just as the father seemed to have developed a fondness for his slave family, the slave family probably held affection for the father.

There are few if any parallels in African American history to the life and career of Wright Cuney. He occupied an unusual position among nineteenth-century black Americans. One striking difference between Cuney and most African American leaders of the era came from his versatility. Whether on the docks of Galveston as the organizer and president of the black Screwmen's Union and as foreman of a screwmen's gang, or serving as alderman on the city council and as commissioner of water, or leading the Texas Republican Party and serving as U.S. collector of customs, Cuney showed considerable talents.

Like all African Americans in nineteenth-century America, North and South, Cuney faced white prejudice. He challenged this by turning the liability of color into an asset. While his leadership sometimes seemed paternalistic in nature, Cuney's charismatic style gained the confidence and support of working-class blacks. One of his most important successes came from his labor activities. When the white screwmen's union, because of racial prejudice, excluded black workers from employment on the wharfs and as members of their union, Cuney convinced white business leaders that he could reduce their labor costs while increasing cotton shipments by using black screwmen to break the white union's monopoly. He then secured guarantees protecting the black presence on the Galveston docks. The subsequent success of black screwmen assured their employment well into the twentieth century.

Cuney learned valuable political skills from his mentor, George T. Ruby. As leader of the Texas Republican Party, Cuney used the numerical advantage of black Republicans to solidify his leadership position and maintaining an African American presence in state politics through the late nineteenth century. Through his practical fusion efforts with other parties, Cuney combined the Republican minority status with other dissident elements to increase black political influence in the state. Although his fusion efforts failed to elect a Republican to statewide office, Cuney forced the Democratic Party to expend valuable political and monetary capital to maintain its position. So great was the threat from the fusionists in the Cuney-Clark campaign of 1892 that many Democrats supporting Gov. James Hogg feared they would lose the election.

Cuney had enormous political skills that he used to gain influence and position within the party. In presidential elections Texas would not be in the Republican column. Cuney knew this as well as anyone, but he refused to let that fact limit the influence of Texas Republicans at the national level. To be influential, the state party had to become a force at national conventions. More often than not Cuney persuaded a majority of Texas delegates to support the eventual presidential nominee of the Republican Party. He added to his influence by creating alliances with powerful party leaders. Because of his effectiveness as a party leader and the alliances he formed, Cuney achieved his personal ambition by receiving the appointment as collector of customs for Galveston and then extended his power and influence within the party through his control of federal patronage in the state.

As an African American political leader, Cuney left a measurable but in some respects problematic legacy. When compared to other black leaders following Reconstruction, Cuney's career appears unequaled. He maintained black control of the state Republican Party and achieved a prominent position in the national organization. He achieved the highest domestic political position allowed to any nineteenth-century African American. Cuney appointed blacks to federal patronage positions under his influence. In Galveston Cuney won election twice as an alderman and became instrumental in protecting and promoting black education. His legacy only becomes problematic when viewed in light of his accomplishments for African Americans generally in Texas. Antagonistic forces beyond his control limited his achievements. No matter how effectively he led the Republican Party, Cuney could not stem the tide of disfranchisement and segregation. His court battles and protest meetings could not halt the erosion of black civil rights. Cuney's place in history remains significant, however, when measured in battles fought as well as in battles won.

Had he lived beyond 1897, Wright Cuney probably would have identified his daughter, Maud, as his most important legacy. No one influenced Maud Cuney more than her father. He provided her with an environment that promoted her intellectual growth while creating pride in her African American heritage. That pride of heritage led her to reject "passing" into white society, which she could have done easily. Wright Cuney helped create the independence of mind that allowed her to leave the harsh seg-regation of the South for the less restrictive North. As an African Ameri-can woman, she refused to accept the roles assigned to either women or blacks in American society. She succeeded outside the home in a profes-sional environment. After her second marriage, Maud Cuney-Hare tran-scended white prejudice to pursue racial uplift. Her ideas embodied the thought of most African American intellectuals in the early twentieth century. Cuney-Hare, her friend W. E. B. Du Bois, and others of the African American elite hoped to create a black community based on educational, literary, artistic, and musical accomplishments that would create a positive black identity.

Cuney-Hare contributed an impressive body of work in pursuit of that goal. She became an important part of the Harlem Renaissance of the early twentieth century. Her musical concerts and lectures brought an awareness of black cultural history to other African Americans. Through her Allied Arts Centre, Cuney-Hare provided an outlet for young black artists, playwrights, actors and actresses, and musicians. Her research, articles, and book *Negro Musicians and Their Music* explored the history of black music and discovered the roots of African American musical heritage. She showed a distinction between black and white cul-ture while revealing the significant contributions made by African Ameri-cans to high culture and American popular culture. Cuney-Hare helped fulfill one of the basic tenants of racial uplift, the creation of black pride in the African American cultural heritage. While she sometimes reflected an elite view of culture, as in her criticism of jazz, Maud Cuney-Hare's research and writing on African American folk music transcended such limitations.

NOTES

CHAPTER I

1. Mary Boykin Chesnut, *A Diary from Dixie,* p. 22; Eugene D. Genovese, *Roll, Jordan, Roll: The World the Slaves Made,* p. 416. Philip Cuney's last name was originally spelled "Cuny" and is first spelled with an added "e" in Texas legislative records and in newspapers of the time. While his white descendants continued the traditional spelling, Philip's black descendants adopted the added "e."

2. Joel Williamson, *New People: Miscegenation and Mulattoes in the United States,* pp. 42–43. Gregg Cantrell, in *Kenneth and John B. Rayner and the Limits of Southern Dissent,* offers a variation on Williamson's maverick idea. He argues that Kenneth Rayner, a North Carolina politician and slaveholder who freed his mulatto son, John, and provided him an education, did so as a dissent from the dominate antebellum views on slavery.

3. G. M. G. Stafford, *The Wells Family of Louisiana and Allied Families,* pp. 144–51.

4. Stafford, *Wells Family,* pp. 146–51; Maud Cuney-Hare, *Norris Wright Cuney: A Tribune of the Black People,* pp. 1–2. Retreating Yankees burned Alexandria's courthouse in 1863, destroying abstracts, land records, and other county records of Rapides Parish. Knowledge of the early settlement of the area consequently comes from secondary materials. Apparently, the marriage of the widow Cuney to Caesar Archinard caused Maud Cuney-Hare to mistakenly identify her grandfather's ancestors as Swiss in the biography of her father. While another source identifies the Cuneys as being of French descent, Stafford's account, which relied on the Cuney family Bible, appears more reliable.

5. J. Frank Dobie, "Jim Bowie, Big Dealer," *Southwestern Historical Quarterly* 60 (Jan., 1957): 342; G. P. Whittington, "Rapides Parish, Louisiana: A History," *Louisiana Historical Quarterly* 18 (Oct., 1933): 629.

6. Whittington, "Rapides Parish," pp. 629–30; William C. Davis, *Three Roads to the Alamo: The Lives and Fortunes of David Crockett, James Bowie, and William Barret Travis,* pp. 212–15. Davis presents the best account of the famous duel, but even his account differs with others on what actually took place.

7. U.S. Census Reports, "Slave Schedules, County of Austin, State of Texas,"
1850, 1860, National Archives, Washington, D.C. (microfilm copies at Lubbock Municipal Library); Ralph A. Wooster, "Wealthy Texans, 1860," *Southwestern Historical Quarterly* 71 (Oct., 1967): 171.

8. U.S. Census Reports, Schedule 4, "Products of Agriculture in the County of
Austin," 1850, 1860, National Archives, Washington, D.C.; "Last Will and
Testament of the Estate of Philip Minor Cuney," Probate Records, Austin
County, Bellville, Tex.; Stafford, *Wells Family*, p. 151.

9. Joyce Martin Murray, ed., *Austin County, Texas: Deed Abstracts, 1837–1852*, pp.
43, 78, 95, 103, 104; "Last Will and Testament of the Estate of Philip Minor
Cuney"; U.S. Census Reports, "Slave Schedules, County of Austin," 1850,
1860; Randolph B. Campbell, *An Empire for Slavery: The Peculiar Institution
in Texas, 1821–1865*, pp. 69, 73–74, 93. Philip Cuney's third wife, Adeline
Spurlock, whom he married in 1849, maintained separate ownership of
twenty-two slaves.

10. *Clarksville Northern Standard*, Dec. 16, 1843, June 25, 28, 1845; "Republic of
Texas Audited Claims," records 1035, 1123, 1184, 2656, Texas State Library
Genealogy Collection, Austin, microfilm reel 23. While the Cuney home no
longer exists, several antebellum homes built in the same style are still in
Austin and Waller Counties.

11. *Journals of the Convention, Assembled at the City of Austin on the Fourth of July,
1845, for the Purpose of Framing a Constitution for the State of Texas*, pp. 16–17,
195–96, 203–204, 207–208, 217–18, 224, 285; Campbell, *Empire for Slavery*, pp.
97, 112.

12. *Biographical Directory of the Texan Conventions and Congresses, 1832–1845*, p.
73; *Journal of the Senate of the State of Texas, First Legislature*, pp. 19, 61, 169,
190–91; "Biographical Sketches," *The Twenty-Seventh Legislature and State
Administration of Texas, 1901*, pp. 92–95. Another Cuney, Philip's grandson,
also served the legislature from Waller County.

13. *Journal of the Senate of the State of Texas, Second Legislature*, pp. 63, 68, 92, 94,
119, 126, 159, 344; "San Felipe De Austin," in *The New Handbook of Texas*, ed.
Ron Tyler and Douglas Barnett, 5:840–41.

14. Roger N. Conger, "The Tomas de la Vega Eleven League Grant on the
Brazos," *Southwestern Historical Quarterly* 61 (Jan., 1968): 372, 376; "Watrous,
John Charles," in *New Handbook of Texas*, ed. Tyler and Barnett, 6:848;
Walace Hawkins, *The Case of John C. Watrous: A Political Story of High
Crimes and Misdemeanors*, pp. 16–17.

15. *Journal of the Senate of the State of Texas, Second Legislature*, pp. 570–71, 598;
Hawkins, *Case of John C. Watrous*, pp. 20–22, 24–27.

16. *Journal of the Senate of the State of Texas, Second Legislature*, pp. 92, 94, 119,
126, 159; Ernest William Winkler, *Platforms of Political Parties in Texas*, pp.
44, 48; *Clarksville Northern Standard*, May 31, 1848.

17. Campbell, *Empire for Slavery*, p. 95.

18. Ibid., p. 195; Herbert G. Gutman, *The Black Family in Slavery and Freedom,
1750–1925*, p. 291.

19. John W. Blassingame, *The Slave Community: Plantation Life in the Antebellum South*, p. 155; Cuney-Hare, *Norris Wright Cuney*, pp. 1–4. Interestingly, Cuney named his fourth mulatto child after Sheriff Wright, who reached his unfortunate end in the sandbar duel.

20. Cuney-Hare, *Norris Wright Cuney*, p. 4; Blassingame, *The Slave Community*, p. 156.

21. Virginia Neal Hinze, "Norris Wright Cuney" (master's thesis: Rice University, 1965), p. 6; Catherine Clinton, *The Plantation Mistress: Woman's World in the Old South*, p. 213.

22. Cuney-Hare, *Norris Wright Cuney*, pp. 3–5; Erasmus Wilson, ed., *Standard History of Pittsburgh Pennsylvania*, pp. 517–18.

23. Cuney-Hare, *Norris Wright Cuney*, pp. 3–5, 10. Of the white Cuney children, Philip Jr. attended the Virginia Military Institute. During the Civil War, he served with distinction in Hiram Granbury's Texas brigade of the Army of Tennessee.

CHAPTER 2

1. Cuney-Hare, *Norris Wright Cuney*, pp. 8–9; David G. McComb, *Galveston: A History*, pp. 85, 88–89.

2. Williamson, *New People*, p. 56. In Texas, which had a smaller number of slaves than most other southern states, mulattoes made up a much smaller number of African Americans.

3. Ibid., pp. 87–89.

4. Cuney-Hare, *Norris Wright Cuney*, pp. 79–81. Many within Galveston's black community found Shakespeare appealing. The "Colored Amateur Shakespearean Dramatic Club" in Galveston often performed for the community, usually under a barrage of white taunts and criticism.

5. Ibid., pp. 82–83.

6. McComb, *Galveston*, pp. 92–93; Cuney-Hare, *Norris Wright Cuney*, pp. 9–10.

7. McComb, *Galveston*, pp. 86–88.

8. Alwyn Barr, *Black Texans: A History of African Americans in Texas, 1528–1995*, p. 66.

9. Willard B. Gatewood, *Aristocrats of Color: The Black Elite, 1880–1920*, p. 212; William H. Grimshaw, *Official History Of Freemasonry: Among the Colored People in North America*, pp. 72–77, 294.

10. Grimshaw, *Official History Of Freemasonry*, pp. 21, 35; George W. Crawford, *Prince Hall and His Followers: Being a Monograph on the Legitimacy of Negro Masonry*, pp. 94–95; William H. Upton, *Negro Masonry: Being a Critical Examination of Objections to the Legitimacy of the Masonry Existing among the Negroes of America*, p. 36; *Toledo Blade*, June 24, 1874, Small Scrapbook, Norris Wright Cuney Collection, Bennett College, Greensboro, N.C., (microfilm, Rice University, Houston). At least one white Masonic leader in Galveston, Jerome Buck, grand master of St. Nicholas Lodge, came out for black recognition. Masonic orders throughout the United States remained segregated.

According to one source, as of 1987 only four African Americans are known members of traditionally white Masonic lodges.

11. Upton, *Negro Masonry,* p. 36.

12. McComb, *Galveston,* pp. 49, 59.

13. Cuney-Hare, *Norris Wright Cuney,* pp. 21–22; "Moody, William Lewis (1828–1920)," in *New Handbook of Texas,* ed. Tyler and Barnett, 4:812.

14. R. L. Fulton, mayor of Galveston, to Pres. Benjamin Harrison, Jan. 5, 1889, Washington, D.C., U.S. Treasury Department Appointment Papers, RG 56, National Archives, Washington, D.C.

15. *Galveston Daily News,* July 31, 1877.

16. Ibid., July 31, Aug. 1, 1877.

17. Ibid., Aug. 1, 2, 1877; Cuney-Hare, *Norris Wright Cuney,* pp. 24–25. Both Virginia Hinze and Maud Cuney-Hare, in their biographies of Wright Cuney, identify Michael Burns as a "white rabble rouser" who threatened violence against the railroad if it did not accede to the strikers demands. But upon close inspection of news reports, he apparently only urged strikers to continue the strike until the railroad was forced to raise wages.

18. James V. Reese, "The Evolution of an Early Texas Union: The Screwmen's Benevolent Association, 1866–1891," *Southwestern Historical Quarterly* 75 (Oct., 1971): 158–61, 164–65.

19. Galveston Screwmen's Benevolent Association [hereafter GSBA], "Minutes," Oct. 5, 1879, Center for American History, University of Texas at Austin, 1:345; Cuney-Hare, *Norris Wright Cuney,* p. 42; Allen Clayton Taylor, "A History of the Screwmen's Benevolent Association: From 1866 to 1924" (master's thesis, University of Texas, 1968), pp. 87–88; *Galveston Daily News,* Mar. 16, 1883.

20. *Galveston Daily News,* Mar. 16, Apr. 4, 1883; Cuney-Hare, *Norris Wright Cuney,* pp. 43–44.

21. GSBA, "Minutes," Apr. 27, 1883; Reese, "Evolution of an Early Texas Union," pp. 181–82; *Galveston Daily News,* Apr. 3, 4, 1883.

22. GSBA, "Minutes," May 11, 1883; Cuney-Hare, *Norris Wright Cuney,* pp. 44–46.

23. GSBA, "Minutes," May 28, June 8, 1883.

24. GSBA, "Minutes," Aug. 27, 1883; *Galveston Daily News,* Oct. 22. 1883; Alwyn Barr, *Reconstruction to Reform: Texas Politics, 1876–1906,* p. 93.

25. Reprint of article from the *New York Sun,* n.d., Large Scrapbook, Cuney Collection. While doing a study of black labor union members in 1900, W. E. B. Du Bois found that, out of a union membership of 1.2 million, less than 40,000 were "nonwhites."

26. Kevin K. Gaines, *Uplifting the Race: Black Leadership, Politics, and Culture in the Twentieth Century,* pp. 94–95; Reese, "Evolution of an Early Texas Union," p. 161.

27. "Address Commemorating Thirtieth Anniversary of Black Emancipation"; and "Address of Hon. N. W. Cuney Before Paul Quinn College Commencement," June 5, 1895, Large Scrapbook, Cuney Collection.

28. Unidentified newspaper article, Apr. 21, 1883, Large Scrapbook, Cuney Collection.

29. Lawrence D. Rice, *The Negro in Texas, 1874–1900*, p. 96; Cuney-Hare, *Norris Wright Cuney*, p. 48; U.S. Census Office, *Compendium of Eleventh Census: 1890*, 1:576; *Galveston Daily News*, Apr. 12, 1885. Some sources list Cuney as a member of the People's party, but this appears to be incorrect.

30. Cuney-Hare, *Norris Wright Cuney*, p. 49; Galveston City Council, "Minutes," Mar. 10, 1883, City Secretary's Office, 6:458–59.

31. *Galveston Daily News*, Mar. 22, 1884. Cuney was not the only African American to serve as Alderman in Galveston. James H. Washington served as alderman from the eighth ward and on the state Republican executive committee. He generally allied himself with Cuney on most council decisions.

32. Galveston City Council, "Minutes," June 4, 1883, 6:564–65, *Galveston Daily News*, June 5, 1883, Oct. 8, 24, Nov. 18, 1884.

33. Fulton to Harrison, Jan. 5, 1889; unidentified newspaper articles, 1886, 1887, Large Scrapbook, Cuney Collection.

34. Galveston City Council, "Minutes," Oct. 7, 20, 1884, 7:259–69; *Galveston Daily News*, Oct. 8, 1884.

35. *Galveston Daily News*, Oct. 18, Dec. 2, 1884.

36. McComb, *Galveston*, pp. 101–102, *Galveston Daily News*, Dec. 14, 17, 1885.

37. Galveston City Council, "Minutes," Nov. 13, 1885, Apr. 22, 1886, May 2, July 5, 1887, 7:600–602, 732–34, 8:168–70, 208–209; McComb, *Galveston*, p. 103; *Galveston Daily News*, n.d., Large Scrapbook, Cuney Collection.

38. *Galveston Daily News*, Apr. 7, 1885; unidentified newspaper article, Apr. 7, 1885, Large Scrapbook, Cuney Collection; Cuney-Hare, *Norris Wright Cuney*, pp. 64–65.

39. *Galveston Daily News*, June 7, 8, 1887.

40. Ibid.

41. Cuney-Hare, *Norris Wright Cuney*, pp. 74–75; *Galveston Daily News*, June 8, 1887.

42. Elizabeth Hayes Turner, *Women, Culture, and Community: Religion and Reform in Galveston, 1880–1920*, p. 230; Cuney-Hare, *Norris Wright Cuney*, pp. 67–68.

43. *Galveston Daily News*, Feb. 29, Mar. 1, 1876. The *Daily News* suggested that "something will have to be done" about Cuney's rash denunciation of Judge Morrill, but no legal actions took place.

44. *Galveston Weekly Argus*, Sept. 11, 1891, Large Scrapbook, Cuney Collection; Barr, *Black Texans*, p. 82; Cuney-Hare, *Norris Wright Cuney*, p. 130.

45. Rice, *The Negro in Texas*, p. 148; *Galveston Daily News*, Oct. 12, 1893; two unidentified newspaper articles, n.d., Large Scrapbook, Cuney Collection.

46. Barr, *Black Texans*, pp. 63, 98.

47. "N. W. Cuney Political Platform," Small Scrapbook, Cuney Collection.

48. Unidentified newspaper article, 1883, Large Scrapbook, Cuney Collection.

49. Turner, *Women, Culture, and Community,* pp. 244–45; *Galveston Daily News,* June 2, 1890, Jan. 8, 1893, Feb. 2, 1894.

50. Unidentified newspaper article, n.d., Small Scrapbook, Cuney Collection; Cuney-Hare, *Norris Wright Cuney,* pp. 32–33.

51. Rice, *The Negro in Texas,* pp. 224–25; *Galveston Daily News,* June 23, 1884.

CHAPTER 3

1. *Houston Post,* Oct. 23, 1888.

2. Cuney-Hare, *Norris Wright Cuney,* p. 8; Barr, *Black Texans,* p. 44; Carl H. Moneyhon, "George T. Ruby and the Politics of Expediency in Texas," in *Southern Black Leaders of the Reconstruction Era,* ed. Howard N. Rabinowitz, pp. 363–66. While working aboard the *Grey Eagle,* Cuney also met P. B. S. Pinchback, the first black lieutenant governor of Louisiana, and they remained friends for the rest of Cuney's life.

3. Barr, *Black Texans,* pp. 44–45; Eric Foner, *Reconstruction: America's Unfinished Revolution, 1863–1877,* p. 283; Moneyhon, "George T. Ruby," pp. 363, 367, 372.

4. James M. Smallwood, *Time of Hope, Time of Despair: Black Texans during Reconstruction,* pp. 136–38.

5. Ibid., 368; Barr, *Reconstruction to Reform,* p. 7; James Alex Baggatt, "Origins of Early Republican Party Leadership," *Journal of Southern History* 60 (Aug., 1974): 441, 452–54; Carl H. Moneyhon, *Republicanism in Reconstruction Texas,* p. 27.

6. Moneyhon, "George T. Ruby," pp. 369–70.

7. Ibid.; Smallwood, *Time of Hope, Time of Despair,* pp. 139–40; Barr, *Black Texans,* pp. 46–47.

8. Smallwood, *Time of Hope, Time of Despair,* pp. 141, 145–46; W. H. Sinclair to C. S. Roberts, Aug. 18, 1868, "Inspection Tour Report, Counties of Jasper, Tyler, Newton, Cherokee, Houston, Trinity, Anderson, Smith, Polk, Rusk, and Walker," Bureau of Refugees, Freedmen, and Abandoned Lands, Record Group 105, National Archives, Washington, D.C., (microfilm, Texas Tech University Library, Lubbock); Moneyhon, "George T. Ruby," p. 372; Douglas Hales, "Violence Perpetrated against African Americans by Whites in Texas during Reconstruction, 1865–1868" (master's thesis, Texas Tech University, 1994), p. 1.

9. Moneyhon, "George T. Ruby," pp. 372–73.

10. Moneyhon, *Republicanism in Reconstruction Texas,* pp. 97–98; Barr, *Black Texans,* p. 47.

11. Moneyhon, "George T. Ruby," pp. 375–77.

12. Cuney-Hare, *Norris Wright Cuney,* p. 13; Moneyhon, "George T. Ruby," pp. 379–80; Moneyhon, *Republicanism in Reconstruction Texas,* p. 159; Barr, *Black Texans,* p. 48.

13. Moneyhon, "George T. Ruby," pp. 379–82.

14. Ibid., pp. 382–84; Smallwood, *Time of Hope, Time of Despair,* pp. 155–56.

15. Moneyhon, "George T. Ruby," pp. 380–82.
16. Ibid., p. 378; Cuney-Hare, *Norris Wright Cuney,* p. 16; Nathan Patton to George S. Boutwell, Feb. 3, Sept. 2, 1873, Galveston; and Nathan Patton to William A. Richardson, July 26, 1873, Galveston, U.S. Treasury Department Appointment Papers, Record Group 56, National Archives, Washington, D.C.
17. Cuney-Hare, *Norris Wright Cuney,* p. 14; *Galveston Daily News,* Oct. 6, 1872.
18. Moneyhon, "George T. Ruby," pp. 385–86.
19. Ibid., p. 388; Smallwood, *Time of Hope, Time of Despair,* pp. 124, 156; Barr, *Black Texans,* pp. 51–52; Winkler, *Platforms of Political Parties,* pp. 149–51.
20. Ronald N. Gray, "Edmund J. Davis: Radical Republican and Reconstruction Governor of Texas" (Ph.D. diss., Texas Tech University, 1976), pp. 363–64.
21. Cuney-Hare, *Norris Wright Cuney,* pp. 27–28; Paul Casdorph, *A History of the Republican Party in Texas, 1865–1965,* p. 35.
22. Hinze, "Norris Wright Cuney," pp. 14–15; R. L. Fulton, mayor of Galveston, to Pres. Benjamin Harrison, Jan. 5, 1889, Washington D.C., Treasury Department Appointment Papers, RG 56; Cuney-Hare, *Norris Wright Cuney,* pp. 27–28. In Hinze's thesis she argues that Cuney may have been a member of the "Poole gang," which became identified with Galveston corruption. This seems highly unlikely since community leaders asked Cuney to participate in the city's reform efforts.
23. Barr, *Reconstruction to Reform,* pp. 20–21; Winkler, *Platforms of Political Parties,* pp. 155, 176–77.
24. G. B. Shields to B. H. Bristow, Mar. 16, May 16, 1876, Galveston; and Edmund J. Davis to Col. Bluford Wilson, secretary of treasury, Apr. 3, 1876, Washington, D.C., Treasury Department Appointment Papers, RG 56.
25. Cuney-Hare, *Norris Wright Cuney,* p. 23; Barr, *Black Texans,* pp. 70–71; "N. W. Cuney Political Platform," Small Scrapbook, Norris Wright Cuney Collection, Bennett College, Greensboro, N.C. (microfilm, Rice University, Houston).
26. Cuney-Hare, *Norris Wright Cuney,* pp. v–vii, 11.
27. Ibid., pp. 17, 19, 28–29.
28. Albert T. Voliviler, ed., *The Correspondence between Benjamin Harrison and James G. Blaine, 1882–1893,* p. 183; William S. McFeely, *Frederick Douglass,* p. 356. Although on many occasions Cuney was an instrumental part of Blaine's national convention strategy, Blaine's public records do not mention him in any substantial way.
29. Leland L. Sage, *William Boyd Allison: A Study in Practical Politics,* pp. 96, 106, 111–12, 144, 239; Barr, *Reconstruction to Reform,* p. 182.
30. Sage, *William Boyd Allison,* pp. 123–24, 143–44.
31. Vincent P. De Santis, "Negro Dissatisfaction with Republican Policy in the South, 1882–1884," *Journal of Negro History* (Apr., 1951): 148–49; Vincent P. De Santis, "The Republican Party and the Southern Negro, 1877–1897," *Journal of Negro History* (Jan., 1960): 72–73.

32. Edmund J. Davis to James P. Newcomb, Austin, Mar. 23, 1877, James P. Newcomb Collection, Center for American History, University of Texas at Austin; Gray, "Edmund J. Davis," p. 381; "Brief of Charges against N. W. Cuney, late Inspector of Customs at Galveston, Texas," Treasury Department Appointment Papers, RG 56. The report seemed hypocritical considering that before civil service reform professional politicians or their friends and relatives filled most patronage positions. F. I. Webb, a friend of Shields and a conservative politician, replaced Cuney.

33. Cuney-Hare, *Norris Wright Cuney*, p. 28; Barr, *Black Texans*, p. 71; Barr, *Reconstruction to Reform*, p. 20.

34. Barr, *Reconstruction to Reform*, pp. 46, 71; Rice, *The Negro in Texas*, pp. 54–57.

35. W. F. Meumer, editor of the *San Antonio Light*, to Norris Wright Cuney, Jan. 16, 1889, Galveston, Letter Press, Norris Wright Cuney Collection, Bennett College, Greensboro, N.C. (microfilm, Rice University, Houston); Rice, *The Negro in Texas*, pp. 55–57; Barr, *Reconstruction to Reform*, pp. 47–48; Casdorph, *Republican Party in Texas*, pp. 38–39.

36. Winkler, *Platforms of Political Parties*, p. 190.

37. Ibid., p. 39; Barr, *Black Texans*, p. 74; "Allen, Richard (1830–1909)," in *New Handbook of Texas*, ed. Tyler and Barnett, 1:112–13; Merline Pitre, *Through Many Dangers, Toils, and Snares: The Black Leadership of Texas, 1868–1900*, p. 174.

38. Nell Irvin Painter, *Exodusters: Black Migration to Kansas after Reconstruction*, pp. 153–56; Barr, *Black Texans*, p. 96; Rice, *The Negro in Texas*, p. 201.

39. "Ellis, William H.," in *New Handbook of Texas*, ed. Tyler and Barnett, 2:833; Edwin S. Redkey, *Black Exodus: Black Nationalist and Back-to-Africa Movements, 1890–1910*, p. 193.

40. Redkey, *Black Exodus*, pp. 22–23; Painter, *Exodusters*, pp. 244–46; Cuney-Hare, *Norris Wright Cuney*, pp. 30–31; Norris Wright Cuney to J. H. Harris, 1889, Texarkana, Tex., Letter Press, Cuney Collection. Cuney left no record of his knowing Booker T. Washington or what he thought of his philosophy. He did have one connection, however, to the famous black leader. Emmett Jay Scott, who became Washington's secretary in 1897 and later secretary-treasurer and business manager of the Tuskegee Institute, was a close friend and ally of Cuney. Scott had worked for the *Houston Post* and edited the *Texas Freedman* before becoming Washington's secretary.

41. Casdorph, *Republican Party in Texas*, pp. 40–42; Barr, *Reconstruction to Reform*, pp. 179–180.

42. Barr, *Reconstruction to Reform*, p. 180; Rice, *The Negro in Texas*, p. 62.

43. Kerek Darren Hogg, "Wash Jones: The Life of George Washington Jones, Economic Radical and Political Dissenter" (master's thesis, Texas Tech University, 1993), pp. 2, 108; Vincent P. De Santis, *Republicans Face the Race Question: The New Departure Years, 1877–1897*, p. 162.

44. *Galveston Daily News*, Aug. 24, 1882; Rice, *The Negro in Texas*, pp. 63–65;

Barr, *Reconstruction to Reform*, p. 180; unidentified newspaper article, Sept. 28, 1882, Small Scrapbook, Cuney Collection; Hogg, "Wash Jones," p. 108.

CHAPTER 4

1. Harold D. Lasswell, *Politics: Who Gets What, When, How*, p. 13.
2. J. Morgan Kousser, *The Shaping of Southern Politics: Suffrage Restriction and the Establishment of the One-Party South, 1880–1910*, pp. 38–40; Barr, *Reconstruction to Reform*, pp. 203–205.
3. *La Grange Dots*, Dec. 15, 1891, Small Scrapbook, Norris Wright Cuney Collection, Bennett College, Greensboro, N.C. (microfilm, Rice University, Houston); James M. Clairborn to Whom It May Concern, n.d., Washington, D.C., U.S. Treasury Department Appointment Papers, Record Group 56, National Archives.
4. *Jefferson Gazette*, July 10, 1884; *New York Sunday Press*, Dec. 18, 1884; and *New York Tribune*, n.d., Small Scrapbook, Cuney Collection.
5. *New York Sunday Press*, Dec. 18, 1884; *New York Tribune*, n.d.; and *St. Louis Republican*, n.d., Small Scrapbook, Cuney Collection.
6. *St. Louis Republican*, n.d., Small Scrapbook, Cuney Collection.
7. *Galveston Daily News*, Apr. 3, May 3, 1884; *Fort Worth Gazette*, Apr. 29, 1884; Cuney-Hare, *Norris Wright Cuney*, p. 56.
8. *Fort Worth Gazette*, May 1, 1884; *Galveston Daily News*, Apr. 30, 1884.
9. Casdorph, *Republican Party in Texas*, p. 51; Cuney-Hare, *Norris Wright Cuney*, p. 56.
10. *Galveston Daily News*, May 1, 2, 1884; *Fort Worth Gazette*, May 1, 2, 1884.
11. *Galveston Daily News*, May 1, 2, 1884; *Fort Worth Gazette*, May 1, 2, 1884; Casdorph, *Republican Party in Texas*, p. 57; Barr, *Reconstruction to Reform*, p. 180.
12. *Galveston Daily News*, May 5, 1884; Casdorph, *Republican Party in Texas*, pp. 47–49; Cuney-Hare, *Norris Wright Cuney*, p. 59.
13. Malcolm Moos, *The Republicans: A History of Their Party*, pp. 166–67; Cuney-Hare, *Norris Wright Cuney*, p. 59; unidentified newspaper article, June 8, 1884, Small Scrapbook, Cuney Collection.
14. *Galveston Daily News*, June 9, 1884; Cuney-Hare, *Norris Wright Cuney*, pp. 59, 62; *Jefferson Gazette*, July 10, 1884.
15. Cuney-Hare, *Norris Wright Cuney*, pp. 61–62; *Jefferson Gazette*, July 10, 1884.
16. Casdorph, *Republican Party in Texas*, p. 49; Rice, *The Negro in Texas*, pp. 40–41; Cuney-Hare, *Norris Wright Cuney*, p. 54; Barr, *Reconstruction to Reform*, pp. 72, 181.
17. Claude H. Hall, "The Fabulous Tom Ochiltree: Promoter, Politician, and Raconteur," *Southwestern Historical Quarterly* 71 (Jan., 1968): 347–48, 369–70; Cuney-Hare, *Norris Wright Cuney*, p. 54.
18. Barr, *Reconstruction to Reform*, pp. 13–14; Hall, "Tom Ochiltree," pp. 349, 364, 365, 369.

19. *Galveston Daily News,* Aug. 27, 1886.

20. Casdorph, *Republican Party in Texas,* pp. 50–53; Barr, *Reconstruction to Reform,* pp. 61–62.

21. Barr, *Reconstruction to Reform,* pp. 86–88; Cantrell, *Kenneth and John B. Rayner,* pp. 192–93.

22. *Fort Worth Gazette,* Sept. 12, 1887.

23. Norris Wright Cuney to James P. Newcomb, Apr. 18, 1887, San Antonio, "General Correspondence, 1879–1887," James P. Newcomb Collection, Center for American History, University of Texas at Austin.

24. Ibid.; Barr, *Reconstruction to Reform,* p. 92; Cuney-Hare, *Norris Wright Cuney,* p. 76.

25. Cuney-Hare, *Norris Wright Cuney,* pp. 69–70; Rice, *The Negro in Texas,* pp.118–19.

26. Rice, *The Negro in Texas,* p. 192; Cuney-Hare, *Norris Wright Cuney,* pp. 70–72.

27. Cuney-Hare, *Norris Wright Cuney,* p. 84; Grimshaw, *Official History of Freemasonry,* pp. 294, 306.

28. Casdorph, *Republican Party in Texas,* pp. 53–54; Rice, *The Negro in Texas,* pp. 121–22; Barr, *Reconstruction to Reform,* pp. 197–98; Cuney-Hare, *Norris Wright Cuney,* pp. 86–87; unidentified newspaper article, n.d., Large Scrapbook, Cuney Collection.

29. Norris Wright Cuney to Hon. George Tichenor, assistant secretary of treasury, Sept. 28, 1889, Washington, D.C.; and Norris Wright Cuney to David Abner, Oct. 29, 1889, Marshall, Tex., Letter Press, Cuney Collection; Cuney-Hare, *Norris Wright Cuney,* p. 90; *Charles M. Ferguson v. J. M. Moore et al.,* case no. 1559, U.S. 2d Circuit Court, Galveston.

30. *Galveston Evening Tribune,* n.d., Small Scrapbook, Cuney Collection; *Fort Worth Gazette,* n.d., Large Scrapbook, Cuney Collection; Cuney-Hare, *Norris Wright Cuney,* p. 95; Norris Wright Cuney to S. A. Shackworth, Nov. 18, 1888, Topeka, Kans., Letter Press, Cuney Collection.

31. Cuney-Hare, *Norris Wright Cuney,* p. 80; Norris Wright Cuney to R. B. Renfro, Oct. 1889, Brownsville, Tex., Letter Press, Cuney Collection.

32. *Galveston Daily News,* Apr. 4, 1888.

33. *Fort Worth Gazette,* Apr. 4, 1884; *Galveston Daily News,* Apr. 3, 4, 1888.

34. *Galveston Daily News,* Apr. 25, 26, 1888; *Fort Worth Gazette,* Apr. 25, 26, 1888; Barr, *Reconstruction to Reform,* pp. 181–82.

35. Homer E. Scolofsky and Allan B. Spetter, *The Presidency of Benjamin Harrison,* pp. 8–9; Sage, *William Boyd Allison,* pp. 206–208, 223, 225–27; *Galveston Daily News,* June 26, 1888.

36. *Fort Worth Gazette,* Sept. 12, 1888; *New York Age,* n.d., Small Scrapbook, Cuney Collection. In Texas Harrison received overwhelming support from the wool industry, which generally favored high tariffs.

37. Cuney-Hare, *Norris Wright Cuney,* pp. 92–93; Rice, *The Negro in Texas,* pp. 66–67; Casdorph, *Republican Party in Texas,* pp. 57–58; Barr, *Reconstruction to Reform,* p. 104.

38. Scolofsky and Spetter, *Presidency of Benjamin Harrison,* pp. 10–12.

CHAPTER 5

1. *Fort Worth Gazette,* Sept. 9, 1896.
2. "Plan of Organization," Headquarters of the Republican Association, Nov. 30, 1888, James P. Newcomb Collection, Center for American History, University of Texas at Austin; *Houston Post,* Oct. 2, 1889.
3. Norris Wright Cuney to Dr. Cochran, Nov. 11, 1888, Letter Press, Norris Wright Cuney Collection, Bennett College, Greensboro, N.C. (microfilm, Rice University, Houston).
4. *Galveston Daily News,* Dec., 1888, Large Scrapbook, Cuney Collection.
5. Scolofsky and Spetter, *Presidency of Benjamin Harrison,* pp. 60–61; Barr, 83; De Santis, "Republican Party and the Southern Negro," pp. 83–84; unidentified newspaper article, 5 Apr. 1889, Large Scrapbook, Cuney Collection; *The New York Times,* Sept. 1, 1889.
6. G. T. Nichols to Mr. President, July 15, 1889, Galveston; R. F. Mann, chairman Republican Executive Committee, to secretary of the treasury, Apr. 18, 1889, Starr, Tex.; and John B. Fallon, president pro tem., Central Republican League Club, to Benjamin Harrison, Apr. 24, 1889, Houston, Treasury Department Appointment Papers, RG 56.
7. W. T. Messmer to Benjamin Harrison, Apr. 9, 1889, San Antonio; Edwin H. Terrell to Benjamin Harrison, Mar. 26, 1889, Washington, D.C.; J. N. Sawyer to Benjamin Harrison, Feb. 13, 1889, Galveston; and R. L. Fulton, mayor of Galveston, to Benjamin Harrison, Jan. 5, 1889, Galveston, Treasury Department Appointment Papers, RG 56.
8. Scolofsky and Spetter, *Presidency of Benjamin Harrison,* pp. 31–32; De Santis, "Republican Party and the Southern Negro," pp. 84–85; Cuney-Hare, *Norris Wright Cuney,* p. 118. If the reports were true, Blaine's advice may not only have represented good politics but also put into question his professed belief in black equality, especially in regard to Cuney, whose loyalty to Blaine was unquestioned.
9. Scolofsky and Spetter, *Presidency of Benjamin Harrison,* pp. 37–38; Cuney-Hare, *Norris Wright Cuney,* pp. 120–21. Clarkson was never shy about self-promotion and probably embellished the story for Cuney's benefit, but the president did send the nomination to the Senate that afternoon.
10. *The New York Times,* July 20, 1889; De Santis, "Republican Party and the Southern Negro," p. 84; unidentified newspaper article, July 20, 1889, Small Scrapbook, Cuney Collection.
11. Barr, *Reconstruction to Reform,* pp. 182–83; Norris Wright Cuney to Hon. E. H. Terrell, ambassador to Belgium, Feb. 19, 1890, Brussels, Letter Press, Cuney Collection.
12. Norris Wright Cuney to J. S. Clarkson, first assistant postmaster general, Oct. 20, 1889, Washington D.C., Letter Press, Cuney Collection.
13. Ibid.; Norris Wright Cuney to F. M. Sutton, Mar. 9, 1890, Beaumont, Tex., Letter Press, Cuney Collection. Early in his tenure as collector of customs, Cuney caused a controversy in Galveston in December 1890 when he

refused to lower the customhouse flags to half-staff upon the death of
Jefferson Davis.

14. Norris Wright Cuney to T. A. Pope, Apr., 1890, Cameron, Tex.; Norris
Wright Cuney to F. P. Clarke, collector of customs of El Paso, Nov. 5, 1890;
and Norris Wright Cuney to J. W. McCree, Mar. 4, 1890, Taylor, Tex., Letter Press, Cuney Collection.

15. Cuney-Hare, *Norris Wright Cuney,* p. 140.

16. *Galveston Daily News,* Sept. 4, 1890; Barr, *Reconstruction to Reform,* p. 184;
Casdorph, *Republican Party in Texas,* pp. 58–60.

17. Scolofsky and Spetter, *Presidency of Benjamin Harrison,* pp. 61–63; Barr, p.
184; Casdorph, *Republican Party in Texas,* p. 59.

18. Norris Wright Cuney to Lock McDaniel, Aug. 24, 1892, Anderson, Tex.,
Letter Press, Cuney Collection.

19. Cantrell, *Kenneth and John B. Rayner,* pp. 204–206.

20. Casdorph, *Republican Party in Texas,* pp. 61–62; Barr, *Reconstruction to Reform,* p. 185; Winkler, *Platforms of Political Parties,* pp. 302–305.

21. *Dallas Morning News,* Feb. 12, 1892.

22. Norris Wright Cuney to R. M. Moore, Aug. 30, 1892, San Antonio, Letter
Press, Cuney Collection; *Fort Worth Gazette,* Sept. 15, 1892.

23. Cuney to Moore, Aug. 30, 1892; Cuney-Hare, *Norris Wright Cuney,* pp.
158–61; *Fort Worth Gazette,* Sept. 15, 1892; Barr, *Reconstruction to Reform,*
p. 136.

24. Cuney-Hare, *Norris Wright Cuney,* p. 160; Barr, *Reconstruction to Reform,* p.
108; Robert C. Cotner, *James Stephen Hogg: A Biography,* pp. 434–35. Hogg's
record on lynching was quite strong. He tried several times to overturn
Texas' manslaughter law, which basically allowed lynchers to go free. It defined such acts as "voluntary homicide committed under the immediate influence of sudden passion arising from an adequate cause."

25. Barr, *Reconstruction to Reform,* p. 138; Grady Stafford, "The Hogg-Clark
Campaign" (master's thesis, University of Texas, 1927), pp. 101–103. 110;
Lawrence Goodwyn, *Democratic Promise: The Populist Moment in America,*
pp. 328–29.

26. Barr, *Reconstruction to Reform,* p. 138; W. M. Stone to James. S. Hogg, Oct. 6,
1892, Burleson County, Tex.; W. S. Fly to Waller S. Baker, Sept. 19, 1892,
Gonzales, Tex.; W. W. Adickes to James S. Hogg, Sept. 21, 1892, Waco; and
E. C. Dickinson to James S. Hogg, Sept. 30, 1892, Rush, Tex., Letters Received, James Stephen Hogg Papers, Center for American History, University of Texas at Austin.

27. Barr, *Reconstruction to Reform,* pp. 137–39; T. U. Lubbock to James S. Hogg,
Sept. 16, 1892, Houston, Letters Received, Hogg Papers.

28. Central Republican League Club to Benjamin Harrison, Jan., 1893, Houston; Sen. Richard Coke to John G. Carlisle, secretary of treasury, Apr. 14,
1893, Washington, D.C.; and Citizens of Galveston to secretary of treasury,
Apr. 3, 1893, Galveston, U.S. Treasury Department Appointment Papers,
Record Group 56, National Archives.

29. L. P. Goddell to James P. Newcomb, May 23, 1894, Fort Worth, Newcomb Collection; Cuney-Hare, *Norris Wright Cuney,* pp. 168–71; Casdorph, *Republican Party in Texas,* p. 63.

30. Winkler, *Platforms of Political Parties,* pp. 336–37; Casdorph, *Republican Party in Texas,* p. 65; Cuney-Hare, *Norris Wright Cuney,* pp. 172–73, Small Scrapbook, Norris Wright Cuney Collection, Bennett College, Greensboro, N.C. (microfilm, Rice University, Houston). Charles Ferguson may have opposed Cuney on the Grant matter for reasons of personal ambition in hopes obtaining a leadership position for him or his brother.

31. Cuney-Hare, *Norris Wright Cuney,* pp. 176–77, 267.

32. H. Wayne Morgan, *William McKinley and His America,* pp. 184–85, 192–93.

33. Cuney-Hare, *Norris Wright Cuney,* pp. 178–80.

34. Sage, *William Boyd Allison,* pp. 264–65.

35. Cuney-Hare, *Norris Wright Cuney,* pp. 182–83; *San Antonio Express,* Mar. 23, 1896.

36. Unidentified newspaper article, Mar. 24, 1896, Small Scrapbook, Cuney Collection; *San Antonio Express,* Mar. 27, 1896.

37. Cuney-Hare, *Norris Wright Cuney,* p. 193; Sage, *William Boyd Allison,* p. 265; Barr, *Reconstruction to Reform,* pp. 186–87.

38. *San Antonio Express,* n.d., Small Scrapbook, Cuney Collection; Cuney-Hare, *Norris Wright Cuney,* p. 199.

39. *Fort Worth Gazette,* Sept. 9, 1896.

40. Cuney-Hare, *Norris Wright Cuney,* pp. 218–20.

41. *Galveston Daily News,* Mar. 6, 1897; Cuney-Hare, *Norris Wright Cuney,* pp. 222–24.

42. *Galveston Tribune,* Mar. 17, 1898.

CHAPTER 6

1. *Pittsburgh Courier,* Apr. 4, 1936.

2. Gatewood, *Aristocrats of Color,* p. 153.

3. Williamson, *New People,* pp. 95, 108–109; Gatewood, *Aristocrats of Color,* pp. 149–50. In discussing racial attitudes in this chapter, special emphasis is placed upon northern racial views since Cuney-Hare made her home there from 1903 until her death in 1936.

4. Gatewood, *Aristocrats of Color,* pp. 151–52, 157.

5. Gaines, *Uplifting the Race,* p. 2.

6. "About Booker T. Washington," in *Up from Slavery,* by Booker T. Washington, collector's ed. (New York: New York Public Library, 1998), pp. xiv–xxi; Gaines, *Uplifting the Race,* p. 38. Washington apparently saw no contradiction in advocating industrial education for other blacks while his own children went, not to Tuskegee, but to two leading black liberal arts colleges, Fisk and Howard Universities.

7. David Levering Lewis, *W. E. B. Du Bois: Biography of a Race, 1868–1919,* pp. 3–4, 11–12, 468.

8. W. E. B. Du Bois, *The Souls of Black Folk*, p. 38; Lewis, *W. E. B. Du Bois*, p. 404; Gaines, *Uplifting the Race*, p. 34; *Gatewood, Aristocrats of Color*, pp. 311–12.

9. Gaines, *Uplifting the Race*, pp. 41–42; Lewis, *W. E. B. Du Bois*, pp. 105–107 (quote, 107); Dorothy C. Salem, ed., *African American Women: A Biographical Dictionary*, p. 443.

10. W. E. B. Du Bois, *The Autobiography of W. E. B. Du Bois: A Soliloquy on Viewing My Life from the Last Decade of Its First Century*, pp. 138–39.

11. Lewis, *W. E. B. Du Bois*, pp. 106–107.

12. Cuney-Hare, *Norris Wright Cuney*, pp. 15, 82–83.

13. *The New York Times*, Aug. 13, 1893; unidentified newspaper article, July 20, 1889, Large Scrapbook, Norris Wright Cuney Collection, Bennett College, Greensboro, N.C. (microfilm, Rice University, Houston); Michael Robert Heintze, *Private Black Colleges in Texas, 1865–1954*, pp. 66–68; Cuney-Hare, *Norris Wright Cuney*, p. 131; Eileen Southern, *The Music of Black Americans: A History*, p. 444.

14. Cuney-Hare, *Norris Wright Cuney*, p. 131; unidentified newspaper article, undated; *Boston Courant*, Oct., 1891; Large Scrapbook, Cuney Collection.

15. *Boston Courant*, Oct., 1891, Small Scrapbook, Cuney Collection; Cuney-Hare, *Norris Wright Cuney*, pp. 131–32.

16. Cuney-Hare, *Norris Wright Cuney*, pp. 132–33.

17. Mark R. Schneider, *Boston Confronts Jim Crow, 1890–1920*, pp. 42–50.

18. Ibid., pp. 50–51; Du Bois, *Autobiography*, p. 139; unidentified newspaper article, n.d.; and *Boston Courant*, Oct., 1891, Large Scrapbook, Cuney Collection.

19. *Boston Courant*, Oct., 1891; and unidentified newspaper article, Nov., 1892, Large Scrapbook; Cuney-Hare, *Norris Wright Cuney*, pp. 133–34; The conservatory apparently never allowed race to become an issue in the future and earned a reputation as a school that welcomed minority students. One of its best-known graduates was Coretta Scott King, who graduated in 1954.

20. Josephine Wright, ed., *New Perspectives in Music: Essays in Honor of Eileen Southern*, p. 378; Du Bois, *Autobiography*, p. 138; Lewis, *W. E. B. Du Bois*, p. 107.

21. Lewis, *W. E. B. Du Bois*, pp. 106–107.

22. Carter G. Woodson, "Maud Cuney-Hare," *Journal of Negro History* 21 (Apr., 1936), p. 239; Josephine Harreld Love, introduction to *Negro Musicians and Their Music*, by Maud Cuney-Hare, p. xx.

23. David Crystal, *The Cambridge Biographical Encyclopedia*, p. 818; Cuney-Hare, *Norris Wright Cuney*, p. 215.

24. Love, introduction, pp. xxi–xxii; Tera W. Hunter, introduction to *Norris Wright Cuney*, by Cuney-Hare, p. xvii.

25. Gatewood, *Aristocrats of Color*, pp. 175–76.

26. Hunter, introduction, pp. xvii–xviii; Cuney-Hare, *Norris Wright Cuney*, pp. 153–54.

27. Paula Giddings, *When and Where I Enter: The Impact of Black Women on Race and Sex in America*, p. 77; James R. Grossman, *Land of Hope: Chicago, Black Southerners, and the Great Migration*, pp. 128–29, 140; Hunter, introduction, p. xviii; St. Clair Drake and Horace R. Cayton, *Black Metropolis: A Study of Negro Life in a Northern City*, 1:50–53; Deborah Gray White, *Too Heavy a Load: Black Women in Defense of Themselves, 1894–1994*, p. 27.

28. Love, introduction, p. xxii; *Chicago Broad Ax*, Sept. 20, 1902. Except for Cuney-Hare's obvious discomfort with her false identity, nothing else is known about other difficulties in the marriage that culminated in divorce.

29. *Chicago Broad Ax*, Sept. 20, 1902, Sept. 17, 1904, Oct. 27, 1907; *Chicago Defender*, Oct. 22, 1907.

30. Carter G. Woodson, "The Cuney Family," *Negro History Bulletin* 11 (Mar., 1948): 125.

CHAPTER 7

1. Maud Cuney-Hare to W. E. B. Du Bois, Boston, Mass., June, 1928, Papers of W. E. B. Du Bois, Archives and Manuscripts Division, University Library, University of Massachusetts at Amherst.

2. Gunnar Myrdal, *An American Dilemma: The Negro Problem and Modern Democracy*, pp. 668–69; Adelaide M. Cromwell, *The Other Brahmins: Boston's Black Upper Class, 1750–1950*, p. 17.

3. Gatewood, *Aristocrats of Color*, pp. 27–28.

4. John Daniels, *In Freedom's Birthplace: A Study of the Boston Negroes*, pp. 140–41.

5. Ibid., pp. 295–97. Fitzgerald's liberal views toward race issues no doubt influenced those of his grandson John Fitzgerald Kennedy when he ascended to the American presidency.

6. Cromwell, *Other Brahmins*, pp. 58–59; Stephen R. Fox, *The Guardian of Boston: William Monroe Trotter*, pp. 4–5, 12–13, 32–35. Following Reconstruction and what he considered the abandonment of black southerners by the Republican Party, James Trotter took the unusual step of joining the Democratic Party. Monroe Trotter continued the family tradition. His newspaper, the *Boston Guardian*, often supported Democratic candidates in Massachusetts and the Northeast.

7. Lewis, *W. E. B. Du Bois*, pp. 315–17, 328, 409.

8. Ibid., pp. 409–411.

9. Daniels, *In Freedom's Birthplace*, pp. 181–82; Gatewood, *Aristocrats of Color*, pp. 110–11.

10. Clarence Cameron White, "Maud Cuney-Hare," *Journal of Negro History* 21 (Apr., 1936): 239–40; Woodson, "Cuney Family," p. 244; W. E. B. Du Bois to Maud Cuney-Hare, Apr. 27, 1932, New York, Du Bois Papers. Both Cameron White and Carter Woodson were longtime personal friends of Cuney-Hare and family. It is not known whether William Hare's pension came from business interests or from government service.

11. Cromwell, *Other Brahmins,* pp. 80–83; Daniels, *In Freedom's Birthplace,* pp. 203–204.

12. Cromwell, *Other Brahmins,* pp. 80–83; Gatewood, *Aristocrats of Color,* pp. 307–308; Daniel, *In Freedom's Birthplace,* p. 204.

13. Maud Cuney-Hare, *The Message of Trees: An Anthology of Leaves and Branches.*

14. Daniel, *In Freedom's Birthplace,* pp. 205–206n; Frank Lincoln Mather, ed., *Who's Who of the Colored Race,* p. 35; Cuney-Hare, preface to *Negro Musicians,* pp. v–vi.

15. Joseph J. Boris, ed., *Who's Who in Colored America, 1928–1929,* p. 390; Cuney-Hare, *Negro Musicians,* pp. 131–32.

16. Mather, *Who's Who of the Colored Race,* p. 230; Cuney-Hare, *Negro Musicians,* p. 364; Southern, *Music of Black Americans,* p. 400; *The New York Times,* Jan. 31, 1919.

17. Maud Cuney-Hare Collection, Woodruff Library Archives, Clark Atlanta University, Atlanta, Ga.

18. Mather, *Who's Who of the Colored Race,* p. 129; *The Crisis,* Sept., 1924, p. 200; Southern, *Music of Black Americans,* p. 250; Cuney-Hare, *Negro Musicians,* pp. 296–97.

19. Concert programs and announcements, Cuney-Hare Collection. The Woodruff Library at Clark Atlanta University holds Cuney-Hare's extensive musical manuscript collection, which includes many rare scores that, according to the library, have received scant recognition from musical scholars. The Schomberg Center for Black Culture in New York City houses Cuney-Hare's musical artifacts and memorabilia.

20. Gaines, *Uplifting the Race,* pp. 76–77.

21. Cuney-Hare, *Negro Musicians,* pp. 159–62, 177.

22. Concert programs and announcements, Cuney-Hare Collection.

23. *The Crisis,* Mar., 1920, p. 338; concert programs and announcements, Cuney-Hare Collection; *Musical America,* Apr., 1920; "Social Progress," *Opportunity: A Journal of Negro Life* 2 (Dec., 1924): 380.

24. *The Crisis,* Mar., 1920, p. 338; *Rochester Democrat and Chronicle,* Apr., 1921, Cuney-Hare Collection; "Preview of Articles," *Journal of Negro History* 31 (July, 1936): 248.

25. Maud Cuney-Hare to W. E. B. Du Bois, Mar. 30, 1924, Boston, Du Bois Papers.

26. Southern, *Music of Black Americans,* pp. 395–96; concert programs and announcements, Cuney-Hare Collection. Because of the extraordinary contributions of people from other cities like Boston and even the southern city of New Orleans, the term "Harlem Renaissance" can be misleading.

27. *The Crisis,* Dec., 1920, p. 78; Maud Cuney-Hare, "Folk Music of the Creoles," in *Negro: An Anthology,* ed. Nancy Cunard, p. 242. Cuney-Hare defined Creoles in musical terms. Traditionally, historians have identified Creoles as Frenchmen or Spaniards born in the Americas.

28. Cuney-Hare, "Folk Music of the Creoles," pp. 243–44; Cuney-Hare, *Negro Musicians,* pp. 235–36; James H. Dormam, ed., *Creoles of Color of the Gulf South* (Knoxville: University of Tennessee Press, 1996), pp. 168–69. While Cuney-Hare dated the migration of blacks from Santo Domingo at 1809, some sources date it to 1791.

29. Cuney-Hare, "Folk Music of the Creoles," pp. 243–44; Cuney-Hare, *Negro Musicians,* pp. 235–36, 265.

30. *The Crisis,* Oct., 1921, p. 259; Cuney-Hare, *Negro Musicians,* pp. 38, 44.

31. *The Crisis,* June, 1924, pp. 64–65; July, 1924, pp. 117–19; Apr., 1925, pp. 258, 260; Maud Cuney-Hare, "Antar of Araby," in *Plays and Pageants from the Life of the Negro,* ed. Willis Richardson, pp. 27–74.

32. Maud Cuney-Hare to W. E. B. Du Bois, Nov. 18, 1924, Boston; and W. E. B. Du Bois to Maud Cuney-Hare, Nov. 21, 1924, New York, Du Bois Papers.

33. Maud Cuney-Hare to W. E. B. Du Bois, Mar. 30, 1924, Jan. 2, Apr. 25, 1925, Boston, Du Bois Papers.

34. Maud Cuney-Hare to W. E. B. Du Bois, May 25, Oct. 19, 1925, Boston, Du Bois Papers; Josephine Harreld Love, introduction to *Negro Musicians,* by Cuney-Hare, p. xxvi.

35. W. E. B. Du Bois to Maud Cuney-Hare, Mar. 12, Dec. 5, 1926 New York.

36. Du Bois, *Autobiography,* pp. 30–31.

37. Maud Cuney-Hare to W. E. B. Du Bois, Dec. 6, 1926, Feb. (?), 1927, Boston; *The Crisis,* Mar., 1927, p. 16.

38. Adelaide M. Cromwell, *An African Victorian Feminist: The Life and Times of Adelaide Smith Casely Hayford, 1868–1960,* p. 131; Jean Elder Cazort, "Maud Cuney-Hare: Musician, Folklorist, Author," in *Notable Black American Women,* ed. Jessie Carney Smith, p. 244; Tera W. Hunter, introduction to *Norris Wright Cuney,* by Cuney-Hare, p. xv. Adelaide Casely Hayford, the wife of Casely Hayford, a barrister-at-law in British West Africa, supplied Cuney-Hare with African artifacts and may have helped with her research of African roots of African American music.

39. *The Crisis,* Mar., 1926, p. 244; Maud Cuney-Hare to W. E. B. Du Bois, Aug., 1928, Boston, Du Bois Papers.

40. W. E. B. Du Bois to Maud Cuney-Hare, Jan. 28, 1927, New York; and Maud Cuney-Hare to W. E. B. Du Bois, Mar. 2, May 2, 1927, Boston, Du Bois Papers.

41. W. E. B. Du Bois to Maud Cuney-Hare, Jan. 5, 1928, New York; and Maud Cuney-Hare to W. E. B. Du Bois, Jan. 2, Apr. 14, 1928, Boston, Du Bois Papers. *The Crisis* printed Joseph Cuney's obituary and photograph. Over the years, Wright Cuney's name came up often in the magazine's articles about Texas. For example, in an article in the issue of October, 1919, on Jim Crow laws, *The Crisis* characterizes Cuney as a "great leader" who had fought the battle for equality in that state.

42. Maud Cuney-Hare, "Portuguese Folk-Songs from Province Town, Cape Cod, Mass.," *The Musical Quarterly* 14 (Jan., 1928): 35–53; Boris, *Who's Who in*

Colored America, p. 211; Giddings, *When and Where I Enter,* pp. 147–48; *The Crisis,* May, 1924, p. 26.

43. Maud Cuney-Hare to W. E. B. Du Bois, Dec. 3, 1929, Feb. 26, 1930, Boston, Du Bois Papers.

44. Maud Cuney-Hare to W. E. B. Du Bois, Mar. 30, May 28, 1930, Boston, Du Bois Papers; Norris Wright Cuney, "Tribute to Haitien Heroism," in *Dessalines: A Dramatic Tale,* by William Edgar Easton, p. 124.

45. Maud Cuney-Hare to W. E. B. Du Bois, July 18, 1930, Boston, Du Bois Papers. Cuney-Hare named the Squantum house Sunnyside after her grandfather's Austin County plantation.

46. Maud Cuney-Hare to W. E. B. Du Bois, Dec. 25, 1930, Feb. 11, 1931, Boston, Du Bois Papers; Boris, *Who's Who in Colored America,* p. 409.

47. Woodson, "Cuney Family," p. 143; "Reviews," *Journal of Negro History* 31 (July, 1936): 220; Southern, *Music of Black Americans,* pp. 259, 444.

48. Cuney-Hare, *Negro Musicians,* pp. 26, 419–23.

49. Ibid., pp. 34–36, 61–62.

50. Ibid., pp. 63–64.

51. Ibid., pp. 63–68.

52. Ibid., pp. 116–22.

53. Ibid., pp. 125–27.

54. Ibid., pp. 95–96, 105–107, 108–11.

55. Ibid., pp. 58, 179–80, 186–90.

56. Ibid., pp. 131–34, 140–44, 153–54, 156. In his review of *Negro Musicians and Their Music,* Carter Woodson wrote that Cuney-Hare "had no patience with untrained youth who wanted recognition before he had developed." One characteristic of jazz is the acceptance and use of improvisation, which did not follow the accepted norms of composition followed by many educated professional musicians at that time. Her attitude may have reflected a bias against such styles.

57. Ibid., pp. 131–32.

58. Ibid., pp. 131–34, 140–44, 153–54, 156. A thorough discussion of jazz and rag-time is beyond this study, however, new scholarship shows that Cuney-Hare, for whatever reasons, misread the meaning of the new music. According to Perry Hall, *In the Vineyard: Working in African American Studies* (Knoxville: University of Tennessee Press, 1999): "The fact that jazz, ragtime, R&B, and other forms have become firmly entrenched in American musical culture in spite of typical resistance and rejection by both whites and mainstream-oriented blacks suggests a kind of authenticity-as a voice for the masses of blacks as well as in terms of maintaining African-derived, distinctly black cultural sensibilities-that mainstream culture fails to negate" (p. 153).

59. Cuney-Hare, *Negro Musicians,* pp. 197, 199–201, 202–203, 237–38. In 1894, on a trip to the United States, Dede's ship sank off the coast of Galveston. Wright and Adelina Cuney opened their home to him, and he remained a guest for two months.

60. Ibid., pp. 239–64; Maud Cuney-Hare to W. E. B. Du Bois, Apr. 22, 1932, Boston; and "Resolution of the American Missionary Association," Mar. 30, 1932, Du Bois Papers.

61. Maud Cuney-Hare to W. E. B. Du Bois, Apr. 22, May 15, Oct. 27, 1932, Boston, Du Bois Papers.

62. Maud Cuney-Hare to W. E. B. Du Bois, July 17, 1932, Boston; W. E. B. Du Bois to Maud Cuney-Hare, Jan. 10, 21, 1933, Chicago, Du Bois Papers. Cuney-Hare did not mention in her letter the identity of the white author who she disagreed with (though a check of the *Mercury* shows him to be George Pullen Jackson). Later, in 1933, George Jackson published *White Spirituals in the Southern Uplands,* which argued that the origins of "Negro Spirituals" came from the white-led Methodist revival movement.

63. Maud Cuney-Hare to W. E. B. Du Bois, Jan. 21, Feb. 1, Mar. 19, Sept. 1933, Boston; W. E. B. Du Bois to Maud Cuney-Hare, Jan. 21, Sept. 14, 1933, New York, Du Bois Papers.

64. W. E. B. Du Bois to Maud Cuney-Hare, Feb. 3, 1934, New York; Maud Cuney-Hare to W. E. B. Du Bois, Jan. 13, 1935, Boston, Du Bois Papers; *The Crisis,* Aug., 1934, p. 245.

65. *Boston Guardian,* Feb. 22, 1936.

66. *The Pittsburgh Courier,* Apr. 4, 1936.

BIBLIOGRAPHY

MANUSCRIPTS AND ARCHIVAL SOURCES

Bureau of Refugees, Freedmen, and Abandoned Lands. Record Group 105, National Archives, Washington, D.C. (microfilm, Texas Tech University Library, Lubbock).

Galveston City Council. "Minutes." City Secretary's Office. Vols. 6, 7, 8. 1883–85.

Galveston Screwmen's Benevolent Association. "Minutes." 2 vols. Center for American History, University of Texas at Austin.

James P. Newcomb Collection. Center for American History, University of Texas at Austin.

James Stephen Hogg Papers. Center for American History, University of Texas at Austin.

"Last Will and Testament of the Estate of Philip Minor Cuney." Probate Records, Austin County, Bellville, Tex.

Maud Cuney-Hare Collection. Woodruff Library Archives, Clark Atlanta University, Atlanta, Ga.

Norris Wright Cuney Collection. Bennett College, Greensboro, N.C. (microfilm, Rice University, Houston).

Papers of W. E. B. Du Bois. Archives and Manuscripts Division, University Library, University of Massachusetts at Amherst.

"Republic of Texas Audited Claims." Records 1035, 1123, 1184, 2656, Texas State Library Genealogy Collection, Austin (microfilm, reel 23).

U.S. Census Reports. Schedule 4, "Products of Agriculture in the County of Austin." 1850, 1860. National Archives, Washington, D.C.

———. "Slave Schedules, County of Austin, State of Texas." 1850, 1860. National Archives, Washington, D.C. (microfilm, Lubbock, Tex., Municipal Library).

U.S. Treasury Department Appointment Papers. Record Group 56, National Archives, Washington, D.C.

BOOKS AND ARTICLES

Baggatt, James Alex. "Origins of Early Republican Party Leadership." *Journal of Southern History* 60 (August, 1974): 441–54.

Barr, Alwyn. *Black Texans: A History of African Americans in Texas, 1528–1995*. 2d ed. Norman: University of Oklahoma Press, 1998.

———. *Reconstruction to Reform: Texas Politics, 1876–1906*. Austin: University of Texas Press, 1971.

Biographical Directory of the Texan Conventions and Congresses, 1832–1845. Austin: Book Exchange, 1941.

"Biographical Sketches." *The Twenty-Seventh Legislature and State Administration of Texas, 1901*. Austin: Ben C. Jones, 1901.

Blassingame, John W. *The Slave Community: Plantation Life in the Antebellum South*. New York: Oxford University Press, 1979.

Boris, Joseph J., ed. *Who's Who in Colored America, 1928–1929*. New York: Who's Who in Colored America, 1929.

Campbell, Randolph B. *An Empire for Slavery: The Peculiar Institution in Texas, 1821–1865*. Baton Rouge: Louisiana State University Press, 1989.

Cantrell, Greg. *Kenneth and John B. Rayner and the Limits of Southern Dissent*. Urbana: University of Illinois Press, 1993.

Casdorph, Paul. *A History of the Republican Party in Texas, 1865–1965*. Austin: Pemberton Press, 1965.

Chesnut, Mary Boykin. *A Diary from Dixie*. Boston: Houghton Mifflin, 1949.

Clinton, Catherine. *The Plantation Mistress: Woman's World in the Old South*. New York: Pantheon, 1982.

Conger, Roger N. "The Tomas de la Vega Eleven League Grant on the Brazos." *Southwestern Historical Quarterly* 61 (January, 1968): 371–82.

Cotner, Robert C. *James Stephen Hogg: A Biography*. Austin: University of Texas, 1959.

Crawford, George W. *Prince Hall and His Followers: Being a Monograph on the Legitimacy of Negro Masonry*. New York: Crisis Press, 1914.

Cromwell, Adelaide M. *An African Victorian Feminist: The Life and Times of Adelaide Smith Casely Hayford, 1868–1960*. London: Frank Cass, 1986.

———. *The Other Brahmins: Boston's Black Upper Class, 1750–1950*. Fayetteville: University of Arkansas Press, 1994.

Crystal, David. *The Cambridge Biographical Encyclopedia*. New York: Cambridge University Press, 1995.

Cuney, Norris Wright. "Tribute to Haitien Heroism." *Dessalines: A Dramatic Tale*. William Edgar Easton. J. W. Burson, 1893.

Cuney-Hare, Maud. "Antar of Araby." In *Plays and Pageants from the Life of the Negro*, edited by Willis Richardson, pp. 27–74. Washington: Associated Publishers, 1930.

———. "Folk Music of the Creoles." In *Negro: An Anthology*, edited by Nancy Cunard, pp. 241–46. London: Wishart, 1934.

———. *The Message of Trees: An Anthology of Leaves and Branches*. Boston: Cornhill, 1918.

———. *Negro Musicians and Their Music*. Washington, D.C.: Associated Publishers, 1936. Reprint, New York: G. K. Hall, 1996.

———. *Norris Wright Cuney: A Tribune of the Black People*. Washington, D.C.: Associated Publishers, 1913. Reprint, New York: G. K. Hall, 1995.

———. "Portuguese Folk-Songs from Province Town, Cape Cod, Mass." *The Musical Quarterly* 14 (January, 1928): 35–53.

Daniels, John. *In Freedom's Birthplace: A Study of the Boston Negroes.* New York: Houghton Mifflin, 1914. Reprint, New York: Negro University Press, 1968.

Davis, William C. *Three Roads to the Alamo: The Lives and Fortunes of David Crockett, James Bowie, and William Barret Travis.* New York: Harper Collins, 1998.

De Santis, Vincent P. "Negro Dissatisfaction with Republican Policy in the South, 1882–1884." *Journal of Negro History* (April, 1951): 148–59.

———. "The Republican Party and the Southern Negro, 1877–1897." *Journal of Negro History* (January, 1960): 71–78.

———. *Republicans Face the Race Question: The New Departure Years, 1877–1897.* Baltimore: The Johns Hopkins Press, 1959.

Dobie, J. Frank. "Jim Bowie, Big Dealer." *Southwestern Historical Quarterly* 60 (January, 1957): 337–57.

Drake, St. Clair, and Horace R. Cayton. *Black Metropolis: A Study of Negro Life in a Northern City.* Vol. 1. New York: Harper and Row, 1962.

Du Bois, W. E. B. *The Autobiography of W. E. B. Du Bois: A Soliloquy on Viewing My Life from the Last Decade of Its First Century.* New York: International Publishers, 1968.

———. *The Souls of Black Folk.* New York: First Vintage, 1990.

Foner, Eric. *Reconstruction: America's Unfinished Revolution, 1863–1877.* New York: Harper and Row, 1988.

Fox, Stephen R. *The Guardian of Boston: William Monroe Trotter.* New York: Athenaeum, 1970.

Gaines, Kevin K. *Uplifting the Race: Black Leadership, Politics, and Culture in the Twentieth Century.* Chapel Hill: University of North Carolina Press, 1996.

Gatewood, Willard B. *Aristocrats of Color: The Black Elite, 1880–1920.* Bloomington: Indiana University Press, 1990.

Genovese, Eugene D. *Roll, Jordan, Roll: The World the Slaves Made.* New York: Vintage, 1976.

Giddings, Paula. *When and Where I Enter: The Impact of Black Women on Race and Sex in America.* New York: Bantam, 1988.

Goodwyn, Lawrence. *Democratic Promise: The Populist Moment in America.* New York: Oxford University Press, 1976.

Gray, Ronald N. "Edmund J. Davis: Radical Republican and Reconstruction Governor of Texas." Ph.D. diss., Texas Tech University, 1976.

Grimshaw, William H. *Official History of Freemasonry: Among the Colored People in North America.* New York: Negro University Press, 1903.

Grossman, James R. *Land of Hope: Chicago, Black Southerners, and the Great Migration.* Chicago: University of Chicago Press, 1989.

Gutman, Herbert G. *The Black Family in Slavery and Freedom, 1750–1925.* New York: Vintage, 1976.

Hall, Claude H. "The Fabulous Tom Ochiltree: Promoter, Politician, and Raconteur." *Southwestern Historical Quarterly* 71 (January, 1968): 347–76.

Hawkins, Walace. *The Case of John C. Watrous: A Political Story of High Crimes and Misdemeanors.* Dallas: University of Dallas, 1950.

Heintze, Michael Robert. *Private Black Colleges in Texas, 1865–1954.* College Station: Texas A&M University Press, 1985.

Hinze, Virginia Neal. "Norris Wright Cuney." Master's thesis, Rice University, 1965.

Hogg, Kerek Darren. "Wash Jones: The Life of George Washington Jones, Economic Radical and Political Dissenter." Master's thesis, Texas Tech University, 1993.

Journals of the Convention, Assembled at the City of Austin on the Fourth of July, 1845, for the Purpose of Framing a Constitution for the State of Texas. Austin: Minor and Cruger, Printers to the Convention, 1845.

Journal of the Senate of the State of Texas, First Legislature. Houston: *Houston Telegraph,* 1848.

Journal of the Senate of the State of Texas, Second Legislature. Houston: *Houston Telegraph,* 1848.

Kousser, J. Morgan. *The Shaping of Southern Politics: Suffrage Restriction and the Establishment of the One-Party South, 1880–1910.* New Haven: Yale University Press, 1974.

Lasswell, Harold D. *Politics: Who Gets What, When, How.* New York, 1936.

Lewis, David Levering. *W. E. B. Du Bois: Biography of A Race, 1868–1919.* New York: Henry Holt, 1993.

Mather, Frank Lincoln, ed. *Who's Who of the Colored Race.* Chicago: N.p., 1915.

McComb, David G. *Galveston: A History.* Austin: University of Texas Press, 1986.

McFeely, William S. *Frederick Douglass.* New York: W. W. Norton, 1991.

Moneyhon, Carl H. *Republicanism in Reconstruction Texas.* Austin: University of Texas Press, 1980.

Moos, Malcolm. *The Republicans: A History of Their Party.* New York: Random House, 1956.

Morgan, H. Wayne. *William McKinley and His America.* Syracuse, N.Y.: Syracuse University Press, 1963.

Murray, Joyce Martin, ed. *Austin County, Texas: Deed Abstracts, 1837–1852.* Wolfe City, Tex.: Henington Publishing, 1987.

Myrdal, Gunnar. *An American Dilemma: The Negro Problem and Modern Democracy.* New York: Harper and Row, 1944.

Painter, Nell Irvin. *Exodusters: Black Migration to Kansas after Reconstruction.* New York: Alfred A. Knopf, 1977.

Pitre, Merline. *Through Many Dangers, Toils, and Snares: The Black Leadership of Texas, 1868–1900.* Austin: Eakin Press, 1985.

Rabinowitz Howard N., ed. *Southern Black Leaders of the Reconstruction Era.* Urbana: University of Illinois Press, 1982.

Redkey, Edwin S. *Black Exodus: Black Nationalist and Back-to-Africa Movements, 1890–1910.* New Haven: Yale University Press, 1969.

Reese, James V. "The Evolution of an Early Texas Union: The Screwmen's

Benevolent Association, 1866–1891." *Southwestern Historical Quarterly* 75 (October, 1971): 158–85.

Rice, Lawrence D. *The Negro in Texas, 1874–1900.* Baton Rouge: Louisiana State University Press, 1971.

Sage, Leland L. *William Boyd Allison: A Study in Practical Politics.* Iowa City: State Historical Society of Iowa, 1956.

Salem, Dorothy C., ed. *African American Women: A Biographical Dictionary.* New York: Garland Publishing, 1993.

Schneider, Mark R. *Boston Confronts Jim Crow, 1890–1920.* Boston: Northeastern University Press, 1997.

Schweninger, Loren. *Black Property Owners in the South, 1790–1915.* Chicago: University of Illinois Press, 1990.

Scolofsky Homer E., and Allan B. Spetter. *The Presidency of Benjamin Harrison.* Lawrence: University Press of Kansas, 1987.

Smallwood, James M. *Time of Hope, Time of Despair: Black Texans during Reconstruction.* Port Washington, N.Y.: Kennekat, 1981.

Smith, Jessie Carney, ed. *Notable Black American Women.* Detroit: Gale Research, 1992.

"Social Progress." *Opportunity: A Journal of Negro Life* 2 (December, 1924): 380.

Southern, Eileen. *The Music of Black Americans: A History.* New York: W. W. Norton, 1983.

Stafford, G. M. G. *The Wells Family of Louisiana and Allied Families.* Alexandria, La.: N.p., 1942.

Stafford, Grady. "The Hogg-Clark Campaign." Master's thesis, University of Texas, 1927.

Taylor, Allen Clayton. "A History of the Screwmen's Benevolent Association: From 1866 to 1924." Master's thesis, University of Texas, 1968.

Turner, Elizabeth Hayes. *Women, Culture, and Community: Religion and Reform in Galveston, 1880–1920.* New York: Oxford University Press, 1997.

Tyler, Ron, and Douglas Barnett, eds. *The New Handbook of Texas.* 6 vols. Austin: Texas State Historical Association, 1996.

U.S. Census Office, *Compendium of Eleventh Census: 1890.* Pt. 1. Washington, D.C.: GPO, 1890.

Upton, William H. *Negro Masonry: Being a Critical Examination of Objections to the Legitimacy of the Masonry Existing among the Negroes of America.* New York: AMS, 1975.

Voliviler, Albert T., ed. *The Correspondence between Benjamin Harrison and James G. Blaine, 1882–1893.* Philadelphia: American Philosophical Society, 1940.

White, Clarence Cameron. "Maud Cuney-Hare." *Journal of Negro History* 21 (April, 1936): 239–40.

White, Deborah Gray. *Too Heavy a Load: Black Women in Defense of Themselves, 1894–1994.* New York: W. W. Norton, 1999.

Whittington, G. P. "Rapides Parish, Louisiana: A History." *Louisiana Historical Quarterly* 18 (October, 1933): 628–34.

Williamson, Joel. *New People: Miscegenation and Mulattoes in the United States.* New York: Free Press, 1980.

Wilson, Erasmus, ed. *Standard History of Pittsburgh, Pennsylvania.* Chicago: H. R. Cornell, 1898.

Winkler, Ernest William. *Platforms of Political Parties in Texas.* Austin: University of Texas, 1916.

Woodson, Carter G. "The Cuney Family." *Negro History Bulletin* 11 (March, 1948): 123–25, 143.

———. "Maud Cuney-Hare." *Journal of Negro History* 21 (April, 1936): 438–39.

———. "Preview of Articles." *Journal of Negro History* 31 (July, 1936): 248–49.

Wooster, Ralph A. "Wealthy Texans, 1860." *Southwestern Historical Quarterly* 71 (October, 1967): 163–18.

Wright, Josephine, ed. *New Perspectives in Music: Essays in Honor of Eileen Southern.* Warren, Mich.: Harmonie Park, 1992.

INDEX

Addams, Jane, 105
African Americans: and black elites, 108;
    and "blue vein" societies, 96; in
    Boston, 109, 111, 116–17; in Chicago,
    105; color consciousness of, 96; and
    Communism, 123; Constitutional
    Convention's failure to protect civil
    rights of, 42; and defiance of Jim Crow
    Laws, 33–34; and disfranchisement,
    70–71; education of, 96; and exodus
    movement, 55; and Great Migration,
    105; and Greenback Party, 53, 54; and
    Louisiana, 119; lynching of, 70; and
    miscegenation, 3–4, 16; and mixed
    race, 16, 95–96; music of, 115–16; and
    northern sentiment, 51; and "passing"
    into white community, 104; political
    sophistication of, 54; and Populist
    Party, 88; and Reconstruction process,
    41, 42; and Republican party, 51–52;
    and Rutherford B. Hayes, 51–52; and
    Texas Loyal Union League, 41; Texas
    population of, 52; and Texas Republi-
    can party, 48, 54, 60; and segregation,
    96; and segregation of education, 36,
    42, 49; and segregation of public
    schools in Galveston, 35–36, 38;
    violence against, 42–43, 70–71; and
    voter registration, 42; and women,
    98–99
African American Methodist Episcopal
    Church, 105
Alderman, Frank Mitchell, 30
Allen, C. J., 32

Allen, Richard: and black exodus
    movement, 54, 55; as candidate
    for Lt. Governor, 54; at state
    convention (1884), 65
Allied Art Centre. *See* Cuney-Hare,
    Maud
Allison, William, 74, 77, 89–90
American Missionary Association, 134
Antarah ibn Shaddad al-'Absi, 121
Archinard, Caesar, 4
Archinard, John, 4
Arthur, Chester A., 57, 63
Atlanta Constitution, 100
Austin County, 6, 7, 8, 15
Austin Opera House, 103

Ball, George, 29
Barr, Alwyn, 52
Bellville, Tex., 8
Biggs and Company, 114
"black and tans," 88
black elite, 111–12, 116
Blaine, James G.: and Benjamin
    Harrison, 74; and black civil rights,
    50; candidacy of (1884),
    63, 65–67, 74, 80; and Credit-
    Mobilier, 51; and Frederick Douglass,
    50–51; and Norris
    Wright Cuney, 50–51, 56; possible
    candidacy of, 56; racial views of, 50;
    as Secretary of State, 50
Blake, Eubie, 133
Blanchard, Alred and Gary, 5
Blassingame, John, 11

Carl Engel, 121–22; and Carter C.
Woodson, 128, 137; and Casely
Hayford, 124; collaboration with
Henry T. Burleigh, 118; and Chicago
settlement work, 105–106; childhood
of, 18, 99, 113; and *Christian Science
Monitor*, 95, 122; and classical music,
115, 116; collaboration with Cameron
White, 113–14, 118; correspondence
with W. E. B. Du Bois, 108, 117–18,
122–23, 125–27, 128, 134–35; and Creole
folksongs, 117, 118–21; and Creole
identity, 119; and *The Crisis*, 95, 118,
121, 122, 123, 125, 135; and Deaf, Dumb,
and Blind Institute for Colored
Youth, 38; death of, 135–36; divorce of,
95, 106; education of, 99, 102;
engagement to Du Bois, 102; and
Ethiopian art, 121; and extended
family, 18, 125; and father's death, 92,
104–105; and father's illness, 92, 95;
financial status of, 112; funeral of, 135–
36; and Galveston hurricane, 125; and
Georgia Douglas Johnson, 126;
graduation from Central High, 37, 99;
and Great Depression, 126; and
Harlem Renaissance, 118; illness of,
95, 122, 125, 134–35; illness of mother,
95; illness of mother-in-law, 122; and
Joseph Cuney (uncle), 125; and
League of Women for Community
Service, 124; and Library of
Congress, 121; and Lloyd Cuney
(brother), 95, 127–28; marriage to
William Parker Hare, 106, 111–12;
marriage to J. Frank McKinley, 104;
and *Mercury*, 134; and Monroe
Trotter, 102; and mother, 99; move to
Boston, 106, 110; move to Chicago,
104; and Musical Arts Center, 122;
musical performances of, 114, 116–17,
121; musical philosophy of, 115–17; and
Musical Quarterly, 126; as a musician,
113; musical reviews of, 104, 114, 117;

and NAACP, 95; and Negro identity,
113; and Nelson Cuney (uncle), 95;
New England Conservatory, 83, 94,
99–101, 102, 106; and *New Music
Review*, 118; and Niagara Movement,
111; and "passing" into white
community, 104–106, 107; and Philip
Cuney, 13; and Portuguese Folksongs,
126; and production of play *Dessalines*,
126–27; publication of *Negro
Musicians*, 136–37; racial pride of, 104–
106, 137; and racial uplift, 94, 121, 132,
137; and racism, 99–101, 102–105, 106,
124, 127–28, 129; recognition by the
American Missionary Society, 134;
recognition by New England
Federation of Churches, 134;
relationship with Du Bois, 94,
102, 107, 118, 123, 126–27, 134–35;
relationship with father, 99, 102–104;
relationship with J. Frank McKinley,
104–106; at Republican National
Convention (1892), 104–105; research
of, 118; and Samuel Coleridge-Taylor
Society, 116; and second home at
Squantum, Mass., 127–28; and South
End Music School, 124; and Soviet
approach to the arts, 123; as teacher at
Prairie View A&M, 106; travels of, 95,
114, 123, 126, 134; and Vera (daughter),
95, 105–106, 113; and view of minstrels,
116; and Wellesley College, 122; and
William Howard Richardson, 94, 114–
15, 117, 125; and William Stanley
Braithwaite, 113, 118
Cuney v. Pullman Palace Car Company
1892, 35–36

Dana, Richard, 101
Davis, Edmund J., 21, 36, 45, 85; African
American support for, 44, 48; and
Chester A. Arthur, 57; death of, 48,
58, 75–76; defeat of, 46–47, 48; elected
governor, 44; dislike of Rutherford B.

ISBN 1-58544-200-3

9 781585 442003

90000